Making Effective Use of Mailed Questionnaires

Daniel C. Lockhart, *Editor*

NEW DIRECTIONS FOR PROGRAM EVALUATION
A Publication of the Evaluation Research Society
ERNEST R. HOUSE, *Editor-in-Chief*

Number 21, March 1984

Paperback sourcebooks in
The Jossey-Bass Higher Education and
Social and Behavioral Sciences Series

Jossey-Bass Inc., Publishers
San Francisco • Washington • London

Daniel C. Lockhart, (Ed.).
Making Effective Use of Mailed Questionnaires.
New Directions for Program Evaluation, no. 21.
San Francisco: Jossey-Bass, 1984.

New Directions for Program Evaluation Series
A Publication of the Evaluation Research Society
Ernest R. House, *Editor-in-Chief*

New Directions for Program Evaluation (publication number
USPS 449-050) is published quarterly by Jossey-Bass Inc.,
Publishers, and is sponsored by the Evaluation Research Society.
Second-class postage rates paid at San Francisco, California,
and at additional mailing offices.

Correspondence:
Subscriptions, single-issue orders, change of address notices, undelivered
copies, and other correspondence should be sent to Subscriptions,
Jossey-Bass Inc., Publishers, 433 California Street, San Francisco
California 94104.

Editorial correspondence should be sent to the Editor-in-Chief,
Ernest House, CIRCE-270, Education Building, University of Illinois,
Champaign, Ill. 61820.

Library of Congress Catalogue Card Number LC 83-82736
International Standard Serial Number ISSN 0164-7989
International Standard Book Number ISBN 87589-782-7

Cover art by Willi Baum
Manufactured in the United States of America

Ordering Information

The paperback sourcebooks listed below are published quarterly and can be ordered either by subscription or single-copy.

Subscriptions cost $35.00 per year for institutions, agencies, and libraries. Individuals can subscribe at the special rate of $25.00 per year *if payment is by personal check.* (Note that the full rate of $35.00 applies if payment is by institutional check, even if the subscription is designated for an individual.) Standing orders are accepted. Subscriptions normally begin with the first of the four sourcebooks in the current publication year of the series. When ordering, please indicate if you prefer your subscription to begin with the first issue of the *coming* year.

Single copies are available at $8.95 when payment accompanies order, and *all single-copy orders under $25.00 must include payment.* (California, New Jersey, New York, and Washington, D.C., residents please include appropriate sales tax.) For billed orders, cost per copy is $8.95 plus postage and handling. (Prices subject to change without notice.)

Bulk orders (ten or more copies) of any individual sourcebook are available at the following discounted prices: 10–49 copies, $8.05 each; 50–100 copies, $7.15 each; over 100 copies, *inquire.* Sales tax and postage and handling charges apply as for single copy orders.

To ensure correct and prompt delivery, all orders must give either the *name of an individual* or an *official purchase order number.* Please submit your order as follows:

Subscriptions: specify series and year subscription is to begin.
Single Copies: specify sourcebook code (such as, PE8) and first two words
of title.

Mail orders for United States and Possessions, Latin America, Canada, Japan, Australia, and New Zealand to:
Jossey-Bass Inc., Publishers
433 California Street
San Francisco, California 94104

Mail orders for all other parts of the world to:
Jossey-Bass Limited
28 Banner Street
London EC1Y 8QE

New Directions for Program Evaluation Series
Ernest R. House, *Editor-in-Chief*

Contents

This chapter describes stages at which the researcher can reduce the resistance of potential respondents to mailed questionnaires.

Editor's Notes

In the 1930s, mailed questionnaires fell into disfavor after sampling biases were shown to be very large. Fortunately, researchers did not stop investigating this methodology, and a continuing process of research and development has served both to revive interest in it and to suggest ways of remedying some of its deficiencies (Rossi, 1982). Improvements in the design of mailed questionnaires have been described in books (Oppenheim, 1966; Alwin, 1978; Bradburn and Sudman, 1979; Labaw, 1980; Dillman, 1978; Erdos and Morgan, 1970) and journal articles (Heberlein and Baumgartner, 1978; McKillip and Lockhart, 1984). Research has concentrated both on the quantitative improvement of return rates and on the qualitative improvement of responses and response accuracy.

This volume, like many others in this series, demonstrates that the Evaluation Research Society (ERS) and Jossey-Bass Publishers, Inc., are taking steps to improve the quality of program evaluation in America. The interest in questionnaire design expressed at recent meetings of the ERS seems to indicate that many evaluators have considered using questionnaires in their evaluations.

This *New Directions for Program Evaluation* sourcebook is designed both for the novice and for the expert user of mailed questionnaires. Chapters One and Two have been included to provide novices with basic information about questionnaire design. Chapters Three, Four, and Five address researchers who are interested in improving the methodology of mailed questionnaires. Chapters Six and Seven attempt to begin a theoretical process by which researchers can test specific hypotheses.

Together, these chapters describe the state of the art in mailed questionnaire design. The existing literature is dispersed among the journals of many disciplines, and there have been few attempts to integrate findings in a document that demonstrates the differences of opinion that characterize scientific endeavors in a free society. This volume recognizes and explores those differences.

The first two chapters are case studies of effective use of the mailed questionnaire methodology. In Chapter One, Altschuld and Lower describe a straightforward evaluation effort that proved to be particularly successful. They tell what they did and why they feel that their study was so successful, and they identify the trade-offs that an individual who is relatively unfamiliar with the methodology must make. In Chapter Two, Russo describes another successful use of the methodology that was also rather unique. The data that he collected were highly qualitative in nature, and respondents were committed to solving a problem by any means necessary. This chapter demonstrates

1

that many fruitful uses of the mailed questionnaire remain to be explored. Russo's example may help to extend our thinking about the methodology.

The next three chapters discuss various aspects of the research on mailed questionnaires. In Chapter Three, Sudman and Bradburn identify cases in which the methodology is particularly applicable, and they address some issues raised by biased answers. Their research typifies recent efforts to compare methodologies in order to determine the methodology best suited to a particular type of study. In Chapter Four, Dillman and colleagues continue Dillman's work on the Total Design Method. In demonstrating the importance of adherence to details of that method, they highlight some important aspects of questionnaire design and provide research evidence bearing on those details. In Chapter Five, Baumgartner and Heberlein review the literature on mailed questionnaires. Their meta-analysis uncovers some interesting trends in recent research.

The last two chapters extend the discussion to theory. While researchers are beginning to take notice of theory in their work, and while certain theories are being actively tested, there is as yet no clear indication of the best direction to follow. Work in this area needs to expand. In Chapter Six, McKillip describes some new theories and defines some testable hypotheses. In Chapter Seven, I outline the behaviors required of respondents to provide researchers with complete and usable questionnaires. The evaluator must develop techniques that facilitate these behaviors in an honest way. By understanding these behaviors first as separate components, then in combination, we can learn how to make the best use of mailed evaluation questionnaires.

Thus, this volume should help all evaluators put the methodology to good use when their work requires mailed questionnaires. It can also help evaluators to determine whether a mailed questionnaire could assist in a particular evaluation effort.

Daniel C. Lockhart
Editor

References

Alwin, D. F. (Ed.). *Survey Design and Analysis of Current Issues.* Beverly Hills: Sage, 1978.

Bradburn, N. M., and Sudman, S. *Improving Interview Method and Questionnaire Design.* San Francisco: Jossey-Bass, 1979.

Dillman, D. A. *Mail and Telephone Surveys: The Total Design Method.* New York: Wiley-Interscience, 1978.

Erdos, P. L., and Morgan, A. J. *Professional Mail Surveys.* New York: McGraw-Hill, 1970.

Heberlein, T. A., and Baumgartner, R. M. "Factors Affecting Response Rates to Mailed Questionnaires: A Quantitative Analysis of the Published Literature." *American Sociological Review,* 1978, *43* (4), 447–462.

Labaw, P. L. *Advanced Questionnaire Design.* Cambridge: Abt, 1980.

McKillip, J., and Lockhart, D. C. "The Effectiveness of Cover-Letter Appeals." *Journal of Social Psychology,* 1984, *122,* 85–91.

Oppenheim, A. N. *Questionnaire Design and Attitude Measurement.* New York: Basic Books, 1966.
Rossi, P. H. "Editor's Notes." In P. H. Rossi (Ed.), *Standards of Evaluation Practice.* New Directions in Program Evaluation, no. 15. San Francisco, Jossey-Bass, 1982.

Daniel C. Lockhart is a research analyst at Hi-Tech Systems, Inc., in Columbus, Georgia.

The procedures used in a successful mailed evaluation questionnaire effort are described in this chapter and guidance is given to those who are unfamiliar with the methodology.

Improving Mailed Questionnaires: Analysis of a 96 Percent Return Rate

James W. Altschuld
Michael A. Lower

Obtaining a high percentage of returned and completed questionnaires is of critical importance to any study that uses a mailed survey technique. Without high return and completion rates, the credibility of survey results can be questioned. Heberlein and Baumgartner (1978) reported that survey return rates vary between an average of 46 percent for one mailing and an average of nearly 84 percent for four mailings. Heberlein and Baumgartner's data were derived from analysis of ninety-eight studies designed to study both return rates and survey methodology. Dillman (1978) provided information about return rates for thirty-eight surveys that used his Total Design Method for developing and implementing mail surveys. The return rates ranged from a low of 58 percent to a high of 94 percent. The surveys encompassed a wide spectrum of topics

The authors acknowledge the Spencer Foundation for its support of the survey study described in this chapter and thank Phyllis M. Thomas for many helpful suggestions concerning the text. Many of the concepts contained in this chapter are modifications of a presentation by the authors at the 1982 annual conference of the Evaluation Network and the Evaluation Research Society in Baltimore.

D. C. Lockhart (Ed.). *Making Effective Use of Mailed Questionnaires.*
New Directions for Program Evaluation, no. 21. San Francisco: Jossey-Bass, March 1984.

5

and samples. The Total Design Method emphasizes careful attention to all details of the survey process, from inception through to completion. It leads not only to high return rates but also to increased completion of items within questionnaires.

Clearly, high questionnaire return and item completion rates can be attained across a variety of situations. Yet, at the same time we suspect that the results given by Heberlein and Baumgartner and by Dillman reflect only a portion of all surveys actually conducted. Indeed, the return rates that they cite are probably much higher than the average for all survey studies. If other survey studies, such as those in unpublished school district or agency reports, were available, the average return rate would be considerably lower. By analogy, we can point to an iceburg, where successful published studies represent the tip and the unpublished studies represent the submerged mass.

Purposes

This chapter has two purposes. The first is to describe a dilemma that confronts those who conduct survey studies who are not survey methodologists. We call it the practitioner's dilemma. The second purpose is to describe the procedures and analyze the return rate results of an unusually successful mail survey that we conducted. In spring 1982, 472 questionnaires dealing with teacher evaluation practices were mailed to a random sample of elementary and secondary principals and teachers in a weighted sample of small, medium, and large school districts in the state of Ohio. The return rate for principals was 100 percent—all 118 questionnaires that we mailed out were returned—and for teachers it was 94 percent—334 questionnaires were returned from the 354 sent. The combined rate was approximately 96 percent. This rate is at the upper extremes of the ranges described by Heberlein and Baumgartner (1978) and by Dillman (1978).

The Practitioner's Dilemma

The mailed questionnaire technique is used extensively in educational evaluation and research studies. In a single area, teacher evaluation, major mail surveys have been conducted by the National Education Association (1964), Stemnock (1969, 1972), Kowalski (1978), Grant and Carvell (1980), and Lower and Altschuld (1982). The technique is well established as a way of collecting information both about educational topics in general and about teacher evaluation in particular.

While the technique is valuable, the results from its use have been somewhat mixed. For example, for all the studies just cited (except that by Lower and Altschuld) in which questionnaires were sent to school district superintendents, return rates varied from a low of 35 percent to a high of 91 percent. One study achieved an overall return rate of 86 percent for administrators and teachers but only at the cost of five follow-up mailings and approximately three and a half months of elapsed survey time. Inspection of the teacher evaluation studies indicates that those sampled were more often administrators—superintendents and principals—than they were teachers. However, this may simply reflect the relative accessibility of educational administrators.

Thus, those who are interested in exploring such educational topics as the evaluation of teaching, a very sensitive area, begin by asking a series of questions: How can the mailed questionnaire methodology best be used? How can return rates be enhanced? How can random samples of administrators and teachers by reached? Herein lies part of the practitioner's dilemma. Such questions as these require the educational evaluator and researcher to become familiar with a body of methodological literature that is extensive, at times statistically complex, and growing rapidly. Survey methodology has become a field in itself that cuts across literature bases in education, sociology, psychology, political science, and other related fields. A very small sample of recent materials includes the texts of Dillman (1978), Bradburn and Sudman (1979), and Sudman and Bradburn (1982) and the comprehensive discussion of survey techniques in needs assessment by Nickens and others (1980). A review of all the texts and research articles in this area would be beyond the practitioner, whose main interest is in the information gleaned from use of the technique, not in the technique itself.

The other side of the dilemma—this issue becomes particularly intense for teacher evaluation and its many related topics—is the concurrent explosive growth of the literature in the substantive area of concern to the questionnaire's user. There are hundreds of articles, manuscripts, and books in an area of concern—teacher evaluation, teacher competency assessment, administration of teacher evaluation procedures, legal issues in teacher evaluation, merit pay, and use of teacher evaluation results, to mention only a few. Thus, the practitioner's dilemma is this: To what extent can he or she obtain substantive expertise in the area to be studied and substantive skills in survey and survey-related techniques?

Procedures

The intent of our study was to ascertain the perceptions and attitudes of principals and teachers in Ohio about the evaluation of teaching. The data collection instrument developed for this purpose was a five or six page questionnaire (five pages for teachers, six pages for principals) that required between twenty and twenty-five minutes of time to complete. Most of the questions were scaled, but space was left at the end of the questionnaire for open-ended response. The questionnaire was divided into six areas: background and general evaluation information, the structure of evaluations, the content of evaluations, use of evaluative information, attitudes toward evaluation, and the strengths and weaknesses of evaluation. The questionnaire was pilot-tested with representative groups and revised prior to use in April, May, and June 1982.

Sampling of public school principals and teachers is always difficult. For example, sampling frames for teachers often do not exist, or they are not easy to obtain. Even when they are, considerable error is possible in the sampling unless school district size is taken into account. Thus, we took seven steps, in the order to be described, to achieve a representative sample and to conduct our study.

First, we organized districts into large, medium, and small strata, based on the number of teachers and buildings in each. Second, we estimated sampling ratio per stratum and selected school systems within strata at random. Third, we sent a mailing to the sixty-three school systems thus selected. The mailing was addressed to the district superintendent. It contained two letters. One explained the nature of the study, and the second was an endorsement of the study by a high-level official of the Ohio Education Department. The researchers stated that they would contact the superintendent by telephone within the week in which he or she received the letter. Fourth, the superintendents or their designates were called on schedule. Fifty-nine school districts agreed through their superintendents to participate in the study. Several asked to review the survey instrument before agreeing to participate. This approval process took as long as six weeks to complete in some cases.

Fifth, as specified in both the superintendent's letter and the subsequent telephone conversation, for each district two principals, one at the elementary level and one at the secondary level, were selected at random from the state directory of school systems. The same directory lists the schools in each system, the administrative staff of each system and the schools within it, and approximate number of student and staff at each school. Only in a few instances did the superintendent object to the principals thus selected. Their suggestions for replacements were always honored. Subsequent to the telephone conversation with the superintendent, building principals were contacted by telephone. The discussion with the superintendent, the nature of the study, and the teacher selection technique were described. Any questions or concerns that the principal had were addressed at this time. Verbal commitment was obtained from all the principals contacted.

Sixth, one week later, the principals received a packet in the mail that contained a cover letter explaining the study, the endorsement letter from the high-level state official, a survey form that they were asked to complete, a stamped and addressed return envelope, and three sealed and numbered packets for teachers. Each of these packets contained a copy of the teacher's questionnaire, a cover letter explaining the study, the endorsement letter, and a stamped and addressed return envelope. Teachers and principals were told that questionnaire data would remain confidential and that data would be analyzed and reported on a group basis. Code numbers were placed on questionnaires to facilitate follow-up requests as necessary. This procedure was explained in the cover letter. Teachers were selected for the study as follows: The state school directory was used to determine the number of teachers per building. Three teachers were selected for each building through a random-number process. One of the random numbers was placed on each teacher packet. Both in the principal's letter and in telephone calls, principals were asked to look at their roster or directory of teachers and count until they reached the first of the three random numbers, the second of the three numbers, and the third. The corresponding packets were then placed in the appropriate teacher's mailbox.

Seventh, district response was monitored as completed questionnaires were returned. If the return rate was low three weeks after the first mailing, the appropriate building principals were called. They generally placed a note of reminder in the teacher's mailbox. In a small number of cases, they placed a follow-up letter prepared by the project staff or a second sealed envelope containing teacher materials in the teacher's mailbox. Follow-up letters plus additional packets as needed were mailed to the principal only after the telephone call.

Return Rate Results

Table 1 summarizes the return rate by school district size, respondent, and school level. As Table 1 shows, the overall return rate was 95.8 percent; that is, of the 472 sampled, 452 responded. For principals, the return rate was 100 percent; all 118 principals returned a completed questionnaire. For teachers, the return rate exceeded 94 percent, and it was consistent across the strata surveyed. This return rate compares favorably with the data examined by Heberlein and Baumgartner (1978) and by Dillman (1978). The average item completion rate exceeded 96 percent, and it was generally consistent across questions.

Table 2 summarizes the return rate by time period. First wave questionnaires were returned within the first three weeks. Second wave questionnaires were returned after follow-up telephone calls and more than three weeks of elapsed time. In developing Table 2, we assumed that materials reached building principals two or three days after the initial mailing and that the teacher packets were placed in the teachers' mailboxes on the third or fourth day. Thus, we allotted approximately one week for distribution and two more weeks for the first wave of returns. The overall first wave return results were high — 82 percent. The rate for principals — 90.7 percent — was slightly higher than the rate for teachers — 79.1 percent. It is possible that additional questionnaires were going into the mail as we were starting the follow-up procedure. In any case, because the second wave was small, comparisons between it and the first wave were judged not to be necessary. Further, due to the extended preliminary discussions with several districts, a few teachers and

Table 1. Percent of Teachers and Principals Responding
by Level of School and School District Size

School District Size	Respondents	Level of School Elementary	Secondary[a]	Total	
Small	Teachers $(N = 108)^b$	94.4	96.3	95.3	(103)[c]
	Principals $(N = 36)$	100.0	100.0	100.0	(36)
Medium	Teachers $(N = 66)$	93.9	93.9	93.9	(62)
	Principals $(N = 22)$	100.0	100.0	100.0	(22)
Large	Teachers $(N = 180)$	94.4	93.3	93.8	(169)
	Principals $(N = 60)$	100.0	100.0	100.0	(60)
	Total $(N = 472)$	95.8	95.8	95.8	$(N = 452)$

[a] Secondary includes junior and senior high schools.
[b] N represents the number of teachers and principals selected to receive the mail survey.
[c] Number of questionnaires completed and returned.

Table 2. First and Second Wave Percent of Response by
District Size and Type of Respondent

School District Size	Respondents	First Wave Return	Second Wave Return	Total	
Small	Teachers $(N = 108)$	75.0	20.4	95.4	
	Principals $(N = 36)$	88.9	11.1	100.0	
Medium	Teachers $(N = 66)$	78.8	15.1	93.9	
	Principals $(N = 22)$	90.9	9.1	100.0	
Large	Teachers $(N = 180)$	81.7	12.2	93.9	
	Principals $(N = 60)$	91.7	8.3	100.0	
	Total $(N = 472)$	82.0	13.8	95.8	$(N = 452)$

Note: First wave questionnaires were returned within three weeks of the initial mailing.
Second wave questionnaires were returned four or more weeks after the initial mailing.

principals did not receive their questionnaires until the middle of May. This late mailing date may have reduced the return rate for some schools slightly.

Analysis of Findings

Retrospective analysis can suffer from inaccurate recollections, inadvertent distortion, selective recall, and deliberate distortion, alone or in various combinations. Since the purpose of our mail survey was not to study return rate and survey methodology per se, the deficiencies of retrospective analysis may indeed be in operation in the paragraphs that follow. However, we did keep accurate records of mailing and return dates and of telephone calls, and these records should help to keep the analysis accurate at least in part. Moreover, a body of related literature provides assistance with post hoc interpretations. Thus, our explanations of our results are based on the available records, on literature bases, and on our best judgment. Table 3 summarizes the elements seen as having contributed to the high rate of return.

Salience. In their analysis of ninety-eight studies that used mailed questionnaire, Heberlein and Baumgartner (1978) found that the importance of

Table 3. Elements Contributing to the High Return Rate of the Evaluation of Teaching Survey

Element	*Description/Comment*
Salience	Importance of questionnaire content to respondent
Timing of the survey study	Decision to conduct survey at a time when many teachers were being evaluated, when principals were involved in conducting teacher evaluations, and when teacher contract decisions were made
Nature of cover letters and endorsement letter	Use of multiple cover letters to contact different actors and endorsement letter designed to gain entree to systems
Procedures for contacting and involving key district personnel	Use of calls to superintendents directly after mailing, starting with the small districts
Central office support	Obtaining central office support or creating the impression of central office support
Bureaucratic structure of school districts	Viewing sampling from the standpoint of structured bureaucracy
Personal telephone contact with principals	Showing strong commitment to the study in those who conduct it
Follow-up procedure	Primarily by telephone
Limited time demands and guaranteed confidentiality	Recognition of and emphasis on the time constraints of respondents; guarantee of confidentiality
Overall attention to detail	Attention to wording of questions, maintenance of schedule, and so forth

the questionnaire topic to respondents greatly enhances the return rate. Dillman and others (1974) suggested that item nonresponse within questionnaires may be a function of the degree to which specific questions relate to the central topic of the questionnaire. In our study, we assumed that the topic — the evaluation of teaching — was salient for both types of respondents, principals and teachers. Evaluation of teaching is thought to be an intensely personal and emotional issue. The evaluation activity itself requires sizable commitments of principal and staff time, and in many cases it has been mandated as a result of negotiations between teacher unions and school boards. For some teachers, their jobs may depend on the outcomes of evaluation. If further testimony about the potential intensity of the topic is needed, we point to the request for proposals issued by the National Institute of Education (NIE) in 1981 (NIE, 1981) to conduct a nationwide study of the evaluation of teaching. In that document, the NIE cited numerous court cases regarding evaluation. The current national debate over merit pay has further enhanced the relevance of the evaluation of teaching. Thus, we consider salience to have been a prime factor affecting return rate in our study. In conjunction with the timing of the questionnaire and with other elements outlined in Table 3, it affected the return rate in a positive manner.

Timing. The salience of issues addressed in our questionnaire may have been heightened by the timing of our survey study. Most teachers are evaluated or informed of evaluation results in March, April, or May. The distribution of our questionnaires coincided with the schedule that many school districts follow for the normal evaluation process. Thus, the topics raised by the questionnaire were of immediate concern both to those being evaluated and to those responsible for the evaluating, and their perceptions can be assumed to have been based on recent experiences. If the questionnaire had been mailed in October or November, we doubt that the return rate would have been as high.

Cover Letters and Endorsement Letter. Our study used three cover letters. Each was less than one page in length. All three letters contained similar descriptions of the study, buy they varied in terms of the information supplied and in their appeals to the recipient. The letter to superintendents asked for district cooperation. Superintendents were told that they would receive a telephone call several days after receiving the letter. The letter also noted the confidential nature of the survey and mentioned the endorsement letter. The tone was one of seeking assistance. Each superintendent was addressed by title and name. The short but very positive endorsement letter on state education department letterhead came from a high-level state education department official who by virtue of his position and specialized duties knew many superintendents on a first-name basis. Many superintendents commented about the endorsement during the telephone calls, and several districts sent us a supportive letter indicating that a carbon copy had been sent to the state education department official who provided the endorsement. Thus, the endorsement letter seems to have been extremely important in gaining entree to the school system, and it cannot be overemphasized. The endorsement letter was also included with the materials sent to principals and teachers, but it seems to have been of less value there, most likely because principals and teachers did not know the individual who supplied the endorsement.

The cover letter to principals resembled the letter to superintendents, but it was not mailed until after the telephone conversations with the principals took place. The principals were thanked for their willingness to participate, and their assistance in the study was reinforced. The letter noted that all responses would be kept confidential, that code numbers were to be used only for keeping track of the survey, and that a summary of results would be sent to participating school districts in the fall. This letter can be characterized as an appeal from the researchers to an individual. It described the teacher sampling process, and it addressed the principal by name and title.

The cover letter to teachers resembled the other two. Slightly greater emphasis was placed on the confidentiality of responses, and the use of code numbers to allow the researchers to communicate with nonrespondents was explained. Since the teachers' names were not available, they were not used in these letters.

Procedures for Contacting and Involving Key Personnel. Our survey strategy used both mail and telephone techniques to contact and involve key personnel. The first mailing to superintendents was followed within three to five days of receipt by a personal call to the superintendent's office. The aim of these calls was to reinforce the concepts and the request contained in the mailing. The first calls were made to small districts, where it was easier to contact the superintendent directly and quickly. Thus, the calls to the larger districts could be made with the knowledge that the small and medium districts had already agreed to participate. This information was conveyed in the later calls to superintendents, where it seems to have influenced some decisions to participate.

Principals were called only after superintendents had committed their districts to involvement. Principals' awareness of district commitment seems to have had a bearing on the 100 percent participation of principals in the study. This is not surprising, Heberlein and Baumgartner (1978, p. 460) noted that "the finding that employees are more likely to return questionnaires may reflect a concern for consequences revolving around a failure to comply with a request." In any case, principal support was critical in obtaining a random sampling of teachers, in distributing materials to selected teachers, and in follow-up.

Since teachers returned completed survey forms in individual envelopes directly to the researchers, it is unlikely that principals were aware of the teachers' responses. Study results revealed several major differences between the responses of teachers and principals (Lower and Altschuld, 1982). This fact, in conjunction with the return rate, suggests that the combination of techniques used in our study was a viable strategy for contacting, involving, and obtaining the cooperation of key personnel.

Central Office Support. Central office support for the project, whether a fact or simply a perception, seems to have been a key factor in the return rate for our study, especially for principals. In turn, central office commitment was at least in part a function of the endorsement letter and of perceived state support for the study. Thus, there was a level-by-level perception of support that followed the bureaucratic structure of education within the state. The relevance of that structure to the study's results is discussed in the next section.

Central office support can be perceived as a form of subtle coercion, and as such it may have an impact both on the return rate and on the responses themselves. Analyses of our data suggest that responses were not affected (Lower and Altschuld, 1982), especially for teachers. The guarantee of confidentiality and anonymity and the method for returning completed surveys seem to have offset the potential impact of coercion on responses.

Bureaucratic Structure. A theme that unites several of the elements just described is the theme of bureaucratic structure. Successful sampling, especially sampling of school systems, building-level principals, and teachers, may depend to a high degree on recognition of the bureaucratic structure in which these individuals operate. Even the sampling frames reflect that underlying order. Our study was undertaken only after we decided to base our sampling strategy on that structure. To make this decision, we asked several questions: How is the cooperation of school systems obtained through superintendents? How is central office support conveyed to staff at the building level? How can we use the building-level structure to contact and involve respondents for whom a sampling frame is not available? In many ways, recognition of the bureaucratic structure of schools and school districts was the cornerstone of our study.

Personal Telephone Contact. Interviews would generally be considered a better means of data collection than mailed surveys were it not for the cost (Dillman and others, 1974). Although the telephone contacts used in our study somewhat increased the cost, they appear to have achieved two important interview-type outcomes that affected the return rate: First, the telephone contacts helped respondents to identify with the researchers. Second, they created a desire in respondents to help the researchers to complete the study. During the second or third phone contact, a number of principals responded to the authors in a positive manner; some even addressed them by their first names.

Follow-Up Procedure. If a school's returns were not complete after three weeks, the principal was called again. As Table 2 indicates, approximately 18 percent of all the questionnaires mailed were still in the field when this telephone contact was made. At the time of these calls, the authors were prepared to send follow-up letters and additional questionnaires to the principal for distribution to teachers. In all but a few instances, this proved to be unnecessary, since the principals stated that they would place a reminder in the teacher's mailbox. Many principals also asked for the random number corresponding to the teacher whose questionnaire had not been received. This seems to indicate that the sampling procedures had been implemented within buildings as designed.

The follow-up procedure extended the contacting and involvement elements that we have already discussed. Capitalizing on these mechanisms, it helped to achieve the 96 percent rate with essentially a single follow-up call.

Limited Time Demands and Guaranteed Confidentiality. Whether the survey instrument is short, medium, or long has practical importance for teachers and administrators. (Sudman and Bradburn address this issue in Chapter Three.) Although research by Lockhart and Russo (1981) indicates that the effects of length on return rate are negligible, the perceived length may have an effect on willingness to participate in studies like ours. In all our verbal contacts with districts, we expressed our concern for length and our resolve not to burden respondents. Administrators reacted favorably to our concern and recognition of it may have influenced their decisions to participate. Such concern is not unique to our study, but the reinforcement may have been, and it may have contributed to our high return rate.

In much the same way, we feel that it was not only the guarantee of confidentiality but the emphasis that we placed on that guarantee that contributed to the high return rate. Both the cover letter and the endorsement letter contained strong statements to that effect, and the guarantee was reiterated in all telephone conversations. Without this emphasis, the return rate might have been lower.

Overall Attention to Detail. Survey research is an overall term for complex, detailed means of collecting data. The process consists of many varied and interactive procedures. The quality of the survey effort and the results achieved cannot be attributed to any one element of that process but represent a cumulative outcome. Our study of the evaluation of teaching reflected the careful attention to detail in survey work that Dillman (1978) advocates. For example, the survey instrument was revised more than five times before we were satisfied that it was ready for distribution. A better understanding of how to write and phrase questions might have reduced this time somewhat.

Inclusion of multiple scales for a single question (Witkin, 1975; Sudman and Bradburn, 1982) proved to be valuable for our study. However, use of this scaling strategy increased the need for close scutiny of the survey items in some instances.

The telephone calls required persistence, especially for busy, large school system administrators. Adherence to schedule was another important facet of our study. Superintendents had to be called shortly after receiving the request for assistance. The facts that many had the cover and endorsement letters close at hand and that they referred to the letters in their conversations with us seem to corroborate this assumption. A delay in calling would probably have reduced the return rate. Thus, both an overall sense of detail and a commitment to full involvement in that detail seem to be necessary conditions for developing and implementing a successful survey study.

Conclusions

To what degree can our findings be generalized to other situations? We think that our findings are highly generalizable to educational studies involving teachers and principals within individual states. First, to reach the target population, it is essential to gain entree to school systems. The bureaucratic structure is a major pathway, starting with the superintendent. High-level state support is important for reaching these superintendents. In virtually every state, a few key state administrators know all the superintendents on a personal basis. If their support for a study can be obtained, system participation should increase and with it the return rate for building-level administrators.

The support of district superintendents is vital for a high return rate in any endeavor, especially a research effort. However, two caveats are in order. Will responses be affected if central office or administrative support is perceived to be coercive in nature? If they are, is the guarantee of confidentiality sufficient to counteract the perceived coercion? We cannot answer these questions. Additional research on return rates and quality of responses is needed for the specific population of principals and teachers if these questions are to be answered.

The importance of salience and survey timing cannot be overemphasized. Such commonsense notions as making hay while the sun shines and striking while the iron is hot apply here. There is no substitute for a questionnaire that respondents perceive to be of high interest and that has been timed to coincide with critical related activities.

Personal telephone contact to enhance return rates in educational surveys is economically feasible within states. Although it increases the time and effort required for conducting the survey, the high return rate that this technique achieves makes it cost-effective. Moreover, our results on this point have been replicated. McColskey (1983), who conducted a mail survey of secondary schools in Ohio, called the principals after they had received the initial study mailing to solicit and reinforce their participation. The first wave return rate was 78 percent, and the total return rate was 84 percent after a single follow-up contact.

The possibility that personal telephone contact with respondents acts as a biasing factor cannot be overlooked. Did the principals in our study participate more than they would have in the absence of such calls? Did a sense of acquaintance with the researchers cause them to respond in a certain way? Did it cause them to push teachers to participate? Will further studies, such as McColskey's, that employ similar techniques be able to achieve high return rates in as cost-effective a manner? If our strategy can be used to collect unbiased responses at a very high rate of return, it certainly merits use in other evaluation and research endeavors.

Many other elements that we have described—the limited time demands on district personnel, the confidentiality, and the follow-up procedures—seem to have had a positive impact on the return rate. Limited time demands and confidentiality are not unique to our strategy, but the degree of emphasis may have been, with the result that principals and teachers perceived us to be sensitive to their concerns. Follow-up procedures were personalized in the same manner.

The last element—overall attention to detail—not only reflects the stance that researchers must take in survey work; it also helps practitioners to understand how to deal with the practitioner's dilemma. We cannot become fully expert in survey methodology, nor can we become fully familiar with the extensive research literature about it, but we can use several of the excellent texts now available to become familiar with the survey as a research tool, we can pay close and careful attention to detail, and we can achieve a high degree of success with surveys in our evaluation and research studies. Thus, our solution to the practitioner's dilemma will be one of reasoned compromise.

To summarize, we suggest that the procedures used in our study can be generalized to other evaluation surveys within public school settings in individual states. Further, application of these techniques should be the object of continued research.

References

Bradburn, N. M., Sudman, S., and Associates. *Improving Interview Method and Questionnaire Design: Response Effects to Threatening Questions in Survey Research.* San Francisco: Jossey-Bass, 1979.

Dillman, D. A., Christenson, J. A., Carpenter, E. H., and Brooks, R. M. "Increasing Mail Questionnaire Response: A Four-State Comparison." *American Sociological Review,* 1974, *39,* 744–756.

Dillman, D. *Mail and Telephone Surveys: The Total Design Method.* New York: Wiley-Interscience, 1978.

Grant, S., and Carvell, R. "A Survey of Elementary School Principals and Teachers: Teacher Evaluation Criteria." *Education,* 1980, *100* (3), 223–226.

Heberlein, T. A., and Baumgartner, R. "Factors Affecting Response Rates to Mailed Questionnaires: A Quantitative Analysis of the Published Literature." *American Sociological Review,* 1978, *43,* 447–462.

Kowalski, J. P. S. *Evaluating Teacher Performance.* Arlington, Va.: Educational Research Service, 1978.

Lockhart, D. C., and Russo, J. R. "The Effect of Length of Questionnaire and Type of Follow-Up on the Return Rate of a Mailed Questionnaire." Paper presented at the annual conference of the Evaluation Network and the Evaluation Research Society, Austin, Texas, October 1981.

Lower, M. A., and Altschuld, J. W. *A Study of Attitudes and Perceptions of the Evaluation of Teaching.* Columbus, Ohio: Ohio State University, 1982.

McColskey, W. H. "Identifying Predictors of Information Utilization by Secondary School Principals." Unpublished dissertation, Ohio State University, 1983.

18

National Education Association. *Evaluation of Classroom Teachers.* Research Report 1964–R14. Washington, D.C.: National Education Association, 1964.

National Institute of Education. *Research on the Development and Use of Teacher Evaluation in Schools.* Request for Proposals NIE-R-81-0019. Washington, D.C.: National Institute of Education, 1981.

Nickens, J. W., Purga, A. J., and Noriega, P. *Research Methods in Needs Assessment.* Washington, D.C.: University Press of America, 1980.

Stemnock, S. K. *Evaluating Teacher Performance.* Educational Research Service Circular No. 3. Washington, D.C.: American Association of School Administrators, 1969.

Stemnock, S K. *Evaluating Teacher Performance.* Educational Research Service Circular No. 2. Washington, D.C. American Association of School Administrators, 1972.

Sudman, S., and Bradburn, N. M. *Asking Questions: A Practical Guide to Questionnaire Design.* San Francisco: Jossey-Bass, 1982.

Witkin, B. R. *An Analysis of Needs Assessment Techniques for Educational Planning at State, Intermediate and District Levels.* Alameda, Calif.: County School System, 1975. (ED 108370)

James W. Altschuld is associate professor in the Department of Education Theory and Practice at Ohio State University.

Michael A. Lower is a graduate student in the Department of Education Theory and Practice at Ohio State University.

This chapter presents two cases in which the mailed questionnaire methodology was used in an applied setting.

Using Mailed Questionnaires in Negotiation Consultation

J. Robert Russo

Data gathering is a major step in any consulting process. A variety of methods have been used to gather data, ranging from full-scale management audits (Alderfer, 1980) to force-field diagnosis (Lippitt and Lippitt, 1978). Mailed questionnaires appear not to have been used as a data-gathering method in negotiation consultation. A traditional search of the literature coupled with a computerized search of the data base uncovered little relevant published material. Corazzini and Heppner (1982) used mailed questionnaires to screen potential members for therapy groups and concluded (p. 224) that information from such questionnaires "serves as a useful resource for the group leaders" during therapy. Information gathered from questionnaires is essential to the success of the negotiation groups that I have guided. In this chapter, I will present two cases that expand on this concept.

Case One: Struggles for Power and Conflict over Turf

In the first case, the major variables were differences in socioeconomic status between and among participants, the narrow self-identities of two major actors, a long history of unresolved conflicts, and a natural boundary — a river — that divided the two groups. As often happens, both groups had an identical pristine purpose; that is, both groups belonged to the same international not-

D. C. Lockhart (Ed.). *Making Effective Use of Mailed Questionnaires.*
New Directions for Program Evaluation, no. 21. San Francisco: Jossey-Bass, March 1984.

for-profit organization. However, the conflict between the two groups had reached proportions that seriously affected their income. Prior to the conflict, the groups had been two of the organization's largest contributing affiliates, and as such they were very important to its success. Moreover, the conflict had become so overt that the organization's image was being damaged in the area represented by the two affiliates.

Clearance by Client. In this case, the parent body sought the aid of a negotiating consultant. The idea that someone from outside might be able to help if the presidents of both groups and their boards of directors agreed originated with the chief executive officer (CEO) of the international organization. He telephoned both presidents to say that a person who could act as such a consultant would be calling to discuss the possibility. In those calls, the consultant indicated that he would engage in negotiations only at the invitation of both parties. During these calls, the idea of a premeeting questionnaire was discussed in general terms, and the importance of information common to the members of both groups was emphasized.

After a series of telephone conversations with the two presidents and the CEO, it was agreed that I would draft an invitation letter to be used by both groups. The thrust of the letter was dictated over the telephone to both presidents, who were to discuss it with members as they selected a date for the meeting from a list of possible dates that they had already agreed on. Parenthetically, it should be noted that the presidents met several times before agreement was reached that the two groups should meet in an attempt to resolve their differences and that these meetings were held on both sides of the river.

Cover Letter. In a situation of this sort, any mailing must use accurate addresses and first-class mail, and recipients must be given about a week's time to reply. My experience had been that individually typed invitations were not an important variable in conflict situations. A follow-up telephone call four days prior to the return deadline helps to personalize the invitation to participate, and it usually comes about a day after the addressee has received the mailing. The letter of invitation used in the case described here read as follows (all identifying material has been deleted):

Local Letterhead

On [day, month, date] a few members of the [   ] and [   ] Chapters will spend the day developing guidelines for joint fund-raising activities. We want to strengthen the cooperation we already have and reduce the potential for creating the kinds of problems we have had in the past. We intend to make this a growth-producing event for all who attend, as well as developing agreements to maximize our future fund-raising efforts in the [geographic] area. The planning has been done with the full involvement of both presidents. The session will be led by Dr. Bob Russo, an organizational consultant who has worked with other units of [   ].

In order to make this day most effective, we have limited direct participation to less than twenty—mostly officers and established board members from each chapter. We want your opinions in advance of the meeting, and as a guide for you we have suggested a few questions on the enclosed sheet. You need *not* limit your comments to these topics. We will duplicate copies of your responses dealing with chapter cooperation and make these available to the participants prior to the meeting.

All comments and suggestions received on or before [a date ten days prior to the meeting] will be included in the premeeting information. Your opinions will be extremely important to the success of this effort. Please take a few minutes to give us your feelings and judgments.

Sincerely,
[Chapter president]

Instrumental Development. After much trial and error and extensive content analysis of premeeeting questionnaires, I have found that the point-counterpoint method of question construction elicits the richest responses. Key word pairs, such as *good-bad, strength-weakness, high-low, top-bottom, best-worse, include-exclude, decrease-increase,* and *too much-too little,* stimulate respondents to express the deepest feelings that they are willing to put into writing and share with other participants. I base this claim on comparisons of respondents' written premeeting responses with their verbal comments during the subsequent meetings.

Most negotiation consultation meetings involve fewer than thirty participants, so open-ended questions are an affordable luxury. When premeeting information is solicited from a larger population, administrators must base decisions about question format on ease of tabulation and analysis.

The content of questions is determined by the results of needs assessment. It is beyond the scope of this chapter to discuss the process and practice of needs assessment; almost any text on organizational consulting will be helpful in this area. The major task in identifying the essential content of questions is one of becoming familiar with the conflict symptoms that are presented and going beyond the presenting symptoms to tease out the essential causes. A reading of the written history—board minutes, reports from past consultants, and internal communications—can be helpful, but the information that these materials provide is limited in the sense that they represent the "formal" positions of participants at a specified earlier time in the organization's history. One rich source of data is interviews with persons who have recently resigned or who have been fired from roles similar to those occupied by parties to the present conflict.

When negotiation is called for, conflict is present. Conflict implies the presence of some scarce commodity—power, money, cooperation, status, area, or control. The roots of conflict and therefore the content of questions can often be identified by using this scarcity model. Other conceptual positions may also be productive (Ford, 1981).

In the case described here, the presenting symptom was a decline in the funds being raised by the two affiliates. The CEO and his staff attributed this decline to two major variables: the presence, first, of one person in each group who needed an excessive amount of personal power and, second, of a natural and historic river boundary between the two groups that they had used to define their turf. In the past, both groups had conducted fund-raising activities. In some instances, they invited each other to participate. This cooperation has moved in both directions across the river. The results were mixed, according to staff of the international office. Their judgment was that the involvement of either of the two major personalities spelled doom to real cooperative efforts. Nonetheless, there was no significantly disruptive conflict until one group hosted a national event across the river in the other group's territory. To exacerbate matters, the international office had offered the event to the other affiliate, but it had rejected it. The event was held, and the two affiliates made the normal attempt at a joint effort. However, a series of problems arose, the details of which are not critical to the purpose of this chapter, that made the conflict between the two groups a concern that warranted outside intervention.

As already indicated, I was invited by the international office to attempt a resolution of conflicts between the two affiliates. The president of each group was consulted by telephone several times. The two presidents were encouraged to meet informally, after it was found that both were aware that one person in each group seemed to be the source of the present problems. As a result of these informal meetings, it was agreed that I would contact both parties and some significant others who could provide background information that might illuminate the present conflict. I made these telephone calls, which were intended to help me construct an effective premeeting questionnaire. I stated this purpose directly to those whom I called. I used point-counterpoint open-ended questions in these telephone interviews and reflective probing to solicit additional information when it seemed needed.

These interviews confirmed the preliminary analysis of situational variables by staff of the international. A major socioeconomic variable also emerged: One of the major personalities was from the very high social class, while the other was from a working middle-class background. Interview data led me to hypothesize that the personality from the high social class invested much of his or her personal identity in his or her affiliation with the organization. For example, that person's name was the only one to appear twice on the official letterhead of the affiliate to which he or she belonged. The difference in social class between these two personalities influenced the type of contributor that each could attract and the type of activities in which each could engage with success. Thus, the preliminary draft of the premeeting questionnaire contained questions dealing with good and poor cooperation and with the nature of projects that the two affiliates conduct in the future. It was agreed that two questions would be added that provided each chapter president with information about members' perceptions of the group, and it was also agreed that this information would not be shared with the other group. All information was to be photocopied, and a complete package was to be sent to every participant one week before the meeting. The questionnaire (with the identifying information deleted) follows:

> The greatest strengths of my chapter are. . .
> In my chapter, the area in greatest need of improvement is. . .
> The most effective cooperation I have ever experienced with the other
>   chapter was when. . .
> The major reason(s) for the good cooperation was (were). . .
> The poorest cooperation I have ever experienced with the other chapter
>   was when. . .
> The major reason(s) for this ineffectiveness was (were). . .
> When we do joint projects with the other chapter in the future, I
>   suggest. . .
> Other comments and suggestions (use additional sheets if necessary)
>
> _____   _____   _____
> Name   Date   Chapter
> All responses received by [date] will be used. An envelope is provided.

Telephone reminders were made to all who had not returned the questionnaire four days before the deadline. In this instance, twenty of twenty-one questionnaires mailed out were returned in usable form before the deadline. The nonrespondent was named in the transmittal letter to prospective participants. The return rate just cited is not unusual in such situations. The interest is high, the potential respondents are well educated, they have been given notice, and they have received a telephone reminder. In addition, the content of the questionnaire is of high emotional content.

Facilitator Summary Report. After the packets sent to participants have been returned, the consultant prepares a summary report for use by the facilitator who conducts the face-to-face negotiations. As with any answers to open-ended questions, a series of categories usually emerges after one reading. Using these categories, the consultant tallies the answers to each question using key words from each respondent. For the purposes of the facilitator, it is important to have at least one direct quote from each participant that he or she can introduce early in the meeting. This indicates to each participant that his or her opinions have been heard. It is beyond the scope of this chapter to describe the process and content of the negotiation sessions themselves.

Postmeeting Questionnaire. Each negotiation session has different content and process outcomes, so each follow-up questionnaire is different in its details, but most questionnaires of this nature resemble the one that follows. I use either the second or the third question, not both. Both produce the same results in a global sense. The third question usually produces reports of positive recall.

Dear Participant in XYZ:

Last [date], you participated in [negotiating session name]. To help assess the effectiveness of that session and to improve the quality of any future activities, please give me your candid opinions.

Sincerely, Bob Russo

Before the workshop, I thought or expected. . .
During the day, the best thing that happened was. . .
The event that stands out in my mind was. . .
Now that I look back, I wish I would have. . .
If a similar event is held in the future, I suggest. . .

Overall, I rate the workshop day 0	10
a total waste	an outstanding experience

Use the other side for additional comments.
Sign your name if you want.

Certain clients and situations require specific follow-up data to justify the cost involved in use of negotiating consultation. In these cases, follow-up questionnaires can take a different form. The second case presented in this chapter used a different kind of instrument. That case involved a two-day session that was to be followed by other meetings of the same group. The reader will notice that the instrument includes its own cover letter. This reduces the apparent volume of the mailing. In informal interviews after a session that I conducted, thirty respondents said that they were more likely to do the questionnaire on receipt because the letter was from someone they knew and because they did not have to turn the page. Again, a stamped addressed envelope should be provided.

Use of Evaluation Results. It is important to have a complete and written understanding on the use of postmeeting results before the session takes place. The use should be determined by client's determination of the organization's needs, by those who pay the consultant's fees, or by both. Ethical guidelines regarding the use of results should be detailed, and they should be understood in advance. For example, are there conditions under which one member of the group could be "sacrificed" for the good of the group as a whole?

I have usually received permission to include one or more questions on the follow-up instrument that allow me to evaluate my own performance. The results may or may not be shared with the client, depending on the prior agreement. I find that this feedback is valuable, especially as consistency develops over time.

Case Two: Former Owners, Now Advisers, Attempt to Control Policy

In the early 1970s, a few energetic parents of children stricken with an incurable disease began an organization to find a cure for that disease. That organization has become a world leader in the medical research community, influencing federal legislation and medical careers. In the beginning, the possibility of a quick cure attracted many adherents. The group grew to more than 100,000 members. As a result of its rapid growth in influence, size, and wealth, the organization became complex, and this complexity created major problems for it. One of the problems involved continuing to tap the expertise of founding members while sharing leadership with newer members and professional staff members. This problem was the focus of the conflict negotiation meetings that involved the use of a premeeting questionnaire and a follow-up instrument.

Clearance by Client. The request for service originated with the executive director of the organization, who was personally experiencing the results of leadership conflict between and among his superiors. Professionals who work for not-for-profits can expect such conflict, but in this case it was interfering not only with daily operations but with the organization's longer-term goals and objectives as well. The volunteer leadership had a formal structure that included a board of directors and an advisory committee. The board of directors had a chairman who was the chief operating officer, and a president who produced the agenda had chaired the board's meetings. In its day-to-day operation, the board used an executive committee format. Its meetings were chaired by the chairman and CEO and had powers of decision making delegated to it by the board. An advisory committee composed of past formal leaders was appointed by the present board chairman. The committee had study and recommending responsibilities but no formal power in policy decisions. Committee members elected the chair.

The problem that the executive director faced was a power conflict between the advisory committee and the board of directors. I always assume when I am called into such a situation that conflict exists. I also assume that the conflict is the result of some scarcity. In this instance, I found that three items were scarce: control of the priority ranking of organizational objectives, social status conferred by power to influence decisions of the executive director for the benefit of selected members, and access to national political figures who had expressed concern for the disease. Identifying the items central to the conflict is the first major task of the questionnaire builder.

Instrument Development. Next, I made a series of telephone calls to parties identified by the executive director as central to the issue. In each interview, I asked my informant to name those whom he or she thought were in the most important positions to help with identification of the major problems and who were most likely to be helpful in providing avenues of resolution. The resulting list was compared with the one provided by the executive director. When I felt that I needed to contact people who were not on the list that the executive director had provided, I sought his clearance. It is very important to maintain open dialogue with the party or parties who contract for the service. (In the data-gathering process that precedes construction of the questionnaire, it often happens that the person who engages the consultant emerges as one of the central figures in the conflict. The use of such information is a professional matter that lies beyond the scope of this chapter. It must suffice to say that feedback must be given to the client in some manner.)

These telephone calls made it clear that the questionnaire construction process would benefit from face-to-face meetings with some of the key actors. Clearance with the executive director was obtained, the added expense was authorized, a schedule was developed, and an itinerary was planned. A series of four face-to-face interviews was conducted over a period of two days. The internal political ramifications of the selection of parties for interviews, the length of time spent on each one, and the sequence of interviews must be evaluated as part of the planning. In this instance, each respondent was told who the others were and why they were selected. Openness and honesty are extremely important in conflict situations. A history of unresolved conflict will produce distorted perceptions, especially among those most involved. Factual information, not rumor or gossip, is what the questionnaire builder must share at this point in the process. He or she is collecting data in order to develop a mailed questionnaire. Rumor and gossip will be made evident in both the results of the questionnaire and as a part of the content of the face-to-face meetings that follow.

In this case, the results of the telephone calls and the face-to-face interviews led me to conclude that a premeeting questionnaire specific to the problem that the executive director had identified would be too threatening to the potential respondents. For example, one of the major problems was the personality and lack of ego strength of the chairman of the advisory committee, and another was the behavior of a past president, who was experiencing an extremely serious personal problem that seemed to exacerbate many of the organizational issues to which he or she was party. Together, the board president, the executive director, and I decided to use a general questionnaire that would allow respondents to disclose as little or as much as they chose. Here is the text of that questionnaire:

What are the major strengths of XYZ?
What are the major weaknesses of XYZ?

XYZ should spend more time, energy, and/or money on...
XYZ now spends too much time, energy, and/or money on...

Signature

Please remember to return this in the enclosed envelope by [date]. Thanks.

Cover Letter. To ensure maximum attendance at negotiating sessions, the meetings were planned for the day and a half before a regular board of directors meetings. This format made possible a subjective, short-term evaluation of the results of sessions. In the past, the conflict at board meetings had reached a point where members walked out and called each other names. Indeed, several board members reported that verbal attacks had become the norm. An emotionally loaded situation of this sort calls for careful management of information flow prior to sessions. Again, it is extremely important for the consultant to be candid and open. In the case described here, the standard cover letter was replaced by the questionnaire, which was mailed to members as part of the notice about the board of directors meeting, at which the advisory committee members would, as usual, be present. Here are the essential sections of that one and a half page letter:

Memorandum

To: Board of Directors and Advisory Committee   Date:
From: President
  [Three short paragraphs regarding the board meetings]
  As a part of our continuing development as an organization, we will devote several hours to a discussion of where XYZ is now, where we are going, and where we should be. These discussions are scheduled to begin with a buffet supper at 5:30–9:30 P.M. on Saturday [date], so that we can include those members of the Board and Advisory Committee who are also involved in the   Committee. We will conclude the discussion on Sunday 8:30–10:00 A.M. prior to the Board meeting. Attendance at both scheduled sessions is extremely important for continuity. These discussions will be facilitated by Dr. Robert Russo, a consultant in the area of organizational development.
  [Travel paragraph] [Hotel paragraph]
  In an attempt to lay the groundwork for our Saturday evening and Sunday morning discussions, please give me your opinions about the present status and future direction of XYZ. I will duplicate all your responses and send the package to all Board members and Advisory Committee members prior to the meeting. All responses received by [date] will be included. You may find the enclosed questions helpful. See you in [   ].

Consultant Summary Report. The package of completed questionnaires was mailed to all prospective participants and to the consultant, who prepared a summary for his own use that quoted each respondent at least once. There were forty prospective participants. From past experience, the organization's officers estimated that approximately thirty, including the key parties to the conflict, would attend, and thirty-two of the forty who received the questionnaire responded after a telephone reminder four days before the deadline. Of the eight who did not respond, four attended, three of whom brought completed questionnaires and gave them to the consultant for duplication prior to the meeting. I have found that listing the names of nonrespondents on the cover letter with the packet of completed questionnaires provides incentive for nonrespondents to comply.

Follow-Up Questionnaire. The intensity and the length of the negotiating sessions in the case described here provided a massive amount of content that needed to be evaluated both during the sessions and after. I used a recording device to dictate an analysis after each session, and I used that material and conversations with the client to develop the follow-up questionnaire that I used in this case:

[Professional letterhead]
[Date]

Members of the XYZ Committee and Board of Directors:

As a professional, I need to continue learning and growing. Your specific feedback about my behavior during the pre–board meeting sessions in [city] will aid me in that growth. The structure below is *not* intended to limit your feedback. You may remain anonymous if you wish. Please check *all* statements that apply to you.

Before the pre–board meeting sessions, I felt that
( )   the questionnaire from [the president] was a waste of time.
( )   the questionnaire was thought provoking.
( )   the pre–board meeting sessions would be a waste of time.
( )   this kind of thing was long overdue.
( )   it was enlightening to read the other's responses to the questionnaire.
( )   other people wrote pretty much what I expected.

During the Saturday evening session, I felt
( )   angry   ( )   relieved   ( )   exhausted
( )   scared   ( )   happy   ( )   upset
( )   sad   ( )   frustrated   ( )   hopeful

During the Sunday morning session, I felt
( )   angry   ( )   relieved   ( )   exhausted
( )   scared   ( )   happy   ( )   upset
( )   sad   ( )   frustrated   ( )   hopeful

Now that I look back to the sessions, I feel that
( )   our time could have been spent on better things than those sessions.
( )   it was just what we needed at the time.
( )   nothing changed because of those sessions.
( )   the board meeting was better because of the sessions.
( )   we should never waste our time and money like that again.
( )   we need to do this kind of thing on a _____ basis.

(regular, semiannual, as-needed)

The event that stands out most in my mind was...
The worst thing was...
The best thing was...
Now that I look back, I wish...
If you conduct a similar event in the future, I suggest...
Overall, I rate the pre–board meeting sessions

0	5	10
a total waste of time	average	an outstanding and productive experience

Thank you for your thoughtful comments. My best wishes for a joyous holiday season,

The two items that consist of adjectives describing feelings have two purposes: First, they provide a check on the facilitator's sensitivity during the meeting. Second, they give the participants an opportunity to identify their feelings in retrospect. This is especially useful, according to nonrandom reports from six of the participants in the case discussed here. Of the thirty-two persons who attended the session, twenty-seven completed and returned the postmeeting questionnaire. How soon after the face-to-face meetings should the follow-up instrument be mailed? I have found that a short time lag seems to increase the return rate and to produce more positive responses.

Summary

When an organization decides that internal conflict has reached levels that warrant the expense of attempting a solution, a consultant is often engaged to conduct negotiations between the parties. In one common method of conflict management, the parties to the conflict are convened for a series of face-to-face discussions in the presence of an outside facilitator (Lippitt and Lippitt, 1978). These discussions consume organizational resources. Lost production, forgone opportunities, and consultant fees are some of the costs of such efforts. Premeeting mailed questionnaires can be used to improve the efficiency and effectiveness of this process. Premeeting questionnaires can complement or replace the usual on-site management audit. Such audits are expensive both in time and money. In some instances, such as the second case described in this chapter, the parties to the conflict were spread across the North American continent.

Furthermore, data collection from mailed questionnaires has several advantages over other forms of data collection. First, the data are collected at the respondents' convenience but within a prescribed time period. Second, the data can be copied and distributed to all prospective participants. Written responses are subject to modification by respondents during the course of the face-to-face meeting. Such modification is the essence of negotiation. In contrast, premeeting data collected by an interviewer during a management audit are subject to public denial even if they are complete and accurate. Distributing the written responses well in advance of the face-to-face meeting allows each participant to become familiar with the positions of others to reexamine his or her position in light of new data from the other participants, and to consider changes in his or her stance.

Construction of the premeeting questionnaire must be based on data. The relevant data are the variables that contribute to the conflict that is perceived to be present. Conflict is created by competition for one or more scarce resources — power, prestige, and so forth. This chapter has discussed sources for such data and the assessment process. I have presented several question forms; the point-counterpoint seems especially effective. Since the populations in the kinds of situation described here are usually quite small, it is often not possible to field test such instruments. However, face validity can be established by asking as many disinterested yet knowledgeable people as possible to examine the final instrument.

The internal political considerations of the process must be considered. For example, in some emotionally loaded situations the order of names in the invitation can be perceived as showing preference for one participant over another. Who signed the cover letter? Who is perceived to have authored the questionnaire? The consultant, the facilitator, and the questionnaire builder must be open and honest with the client. If rumor and gossip were not already rampant, the negotiation process would not be needed. Rumor and gossip will constitute much of the agenda for the face-to-face meetings.

It is important to place premeeting understandings with the client in writing. The nature of follow-up activities must be specified. Mailed evaluation questionnaires, summary results, lists of who gets what data, and schedules for data collection all need to be agreed upon before follow-up activities are planned. In my experience, mailed questionnaires are a valuable tool for such follow-up.

References

Alderfer, C. P. "The Methodology of Organizational Diagnosis." *Professional Psychology,* 1980, *11* (3).
Corazzini, J., and Heppner, P. "Client-Therapist Preparation of Group Therapy: Expanding the Diagnostic Interview." *Small Group Behavior,* 1982, 13 (2).

Ford, J. "The Management of Organizational Crises." *Business Horizons,* 1981, *24* (3).

Lippitt, G., and Lippitt, R. *The Consulting Process in Action.* La Jolla, Calif.: University Associates, 1978.

J. Robert Russo is professor of psychology, Southern Illinois University at Edwardsville.

*The authors identify situations in which mailed questionnaires
are most appropriate. Population variables, characteristics
of questionnaires, and social desireability variables are
examined in depth.*

Improving Mailed
Questionnaire Design

Seymour Sudman
Norman Bradburn

Mailed questionnaires can be a powerful tool both in policy formulation and
in evaluation if they are used appropriately. This chapter identifies the situations in which mailed questionnaires are most appropriate and those in which
more expensive procedures are necessary. We steer a middle course between
those who feel that all data worth gathering can be obtained by mail and those
who doubt that mail can ever be satisfactory.

Mail procedures are almost always less costly than personal procedures, although, as other chapters note, careful mail surveys require several
mailings, and they may also require some personal follow-up. In any case, no
one is interested in buying unsatisfactory results at a low price. When mail
procedures are used appropriately, they can be expected to produce results
ranging from almost as good as to substantially better than those that can be
obtained by more costly methods.

However, all is not lost if mail methods are inappropriate. Even with
limited budgets, policy evaluation is possible if personal interviews can be conducted by existing staff or volunteers. Although samples may have to be small,
a small, carefully selected sample is preferable to a large, biased sample. Thus,
the first part of this chapter discusses the situations in which mailed questionnaires can be expected to yield high sample cooperation and low sample

D. C. Lockhart (Ed.). *Making Effective Use of Mailed Questionnaires.*
New Directions for Program Evaluation, no. 21. San Francisco: Jossey-Bass, March 1984.

biases. Cooperation has two major determinants: the nature of the population being studied and the length and characteristics of the questionnaire.

Even if cooperation is satisfactory, the content of the questionnaire is critical in determining whether it should be mailed. Some kinds of questions can be answered better by mail, while other kinds are difficult or impossible to answer by mail. For many questions, however, it makes no difference whether mail or personal methods are used, and when there is no difference, mail methods are preferable if sample cooperation is adequate.

One more factor must be considered before it can be decided whether to use mailed questionnaires — the time available. Mailed surveys require several months to do well, since time must be allowed for multiple mailings, for delivery in both directions, and for recipients to read, complete, and return the questionnaire. If the policy evaluator faces a tight deadline, mail methods may be too time-consuming.

Populations for Which Mail Surveys Are Appropriate

Not all program evaluations involve the general public. Many involve special groups, such as members of a professional society or recipients of printed information. Such special groups are especially appropriate for mailed surveys. Table 1 lists cooperation rates for a variety of special populations derived from reports on these studies in professional journals.

Cooperation rates for these populations range from 88 percent to about 50 percent. Most of the cooperation rates displayed in Table 1 could not be improved by use of personal interviewing procedures. A special comment should be made about physicians. Becuase of their busy schedules and the number of questionnaires that they receive, the response rate for physicians tends to be lower than the rates for most other professional groups, except when physicians perceive the study as being especially salient to their specialties.

The high cooperation rate that can be obtained from most special groups depends on three factors: First, the educational level of these groups is

Table 1. Cooperation Rates on Mail Surveys for Members of Professional Groups or Special Populations

Physician AMA PSP	80–50% (1966–78)
Accountants	81%
Attorneys	67–65% (1975–82)
Teachers	88–71%
Dentists	63%
Dental hygienists not belonging to ADHA	62%
Dental hygienists belonging to ADHA	76%

higher than that of the general population, and members of these groups have substantial experience with forms and questionnaires. Second, the questionnaires usually deal with topics closely related to the professional activities of recipients, and thus they are perceived as interesting and relevant. Third, members of these groups often lead busy lives, and they are difficult to pin down for a personal interview, but they can complete a mailed questionnaire at their own convenience.

Populations for Which Mail Surveys Are Not Appropriate

Just as some respondents find mail surveys particularly easy and interesting, other groups, especially those whose members are aged or who have less education, find mail surveys difficult. We do not present a table showing the low rates of cooperation obtained by mail surveys of these groups, because examples are not to be found in the published sources. Researchers either have avoided using mail for such groups, or low cooperation rates have made it difficult to get results published. There are two reasons why mail is generally unsatisfactory for these groups: First, they find the questionnaire hard to read and to understand. They are concerned that they will make mistakes in answering the questions and that they will appear foolish to the person who reads their answers. Second, they have little or no experience with questionnaires, and they may be uncertain or suspicious of the study itself. Populations for which mailed questionnaires are not appropriate can be interviewed, or someone can hand and explain questionnaires to their members. The second method is especially appropriate at facilities that provide a medical or social service that wish to have service recipients evaluate the service. There is one problem with this procedure: The reactions are likely to be slightly more favorable at the service site than they are if the interview is conducted in the recipient's home. Nevertheless, the procedure of handing out a form at the site is generally superior to mailing if the survey population consists of the aged or the less-educated.

Mail Surveys of the General Population

The greatest uncertainty lies in the use of mailed questionnaires with the general population. In the past, it was felt that the cooperation rate was so low for mail surveys of the general population that mail could not be used. However, recent research by Dillman (1978) and others makes it clear that mailed questionnaires can be used with the general population if the questionnaires are sufficiently short and simple and if the topic has some salience. Two major reasons for the increased use of mail procedures is the increased level of education among the general public and the public's increasing familiarity with forms of all types. Of course, the improvements in mail procedures discussed in this volume have also been important in increasing cooperation.

Nevertheless, cooperation rates are still lower for the general public than they are for special professional groups, and they are lower than the rates that can be obtained from the general public using personal procedures. Table 2 gives estimates of cooperation with a wide range of mail surveys of the general public. These rates range from about 54 percent to 77 percent when adjusted to account for households not on sampling lists. While these rates are 10 to 20 percent lower than can be obtained from the same populations with personal interviews, they are still sufficiently high to be useful for many program evaluations.

The cooperation rates given in Table 2 do not include results for the largest cities and metropolitan areas. Cooperation rates in these places are below average for personal interviews, and we can expect that they would be below average for mail questionnaires, because such areas generally contain large numbers of respondents whose native languages are not English. Moreover, there is greater suspicion of surveys and less willingness to cooperate in cities than there is in towns or rural areas. As a result, city officials in New York, Chicago, or another of the twenty largest cities would have great difficulty in conducting a mail survey for purposes of program evaluation. However, officials in smaller communities will usually find above-average cooperation for their mail surveys unless language is a problem.

Checking for Potential Sample Biases

As in all methods of data collection, the user should make every reasonable effort to compare the characteristics of the sample reached by mail with characteristics of the total population known from census data or other sources. The absence of differences on demographic variables is reassuring, but it does not guarantee that there will be no differences on nondemographic variables. The most accurate but also the most costly way of checking for potential sample biases is to use telephone or face-to-face procedures to contact a subsample of noncooperators with the mail survey. If no differences are

Table 2. Cooperation Rates on Mail Surveys for General Populations

Washington state	68%
Seattle, Washington	54%
North Carolina	63%
Arizona	64%
Indiana	64%
Iowa	70%
Michigan	61%
Kentucky	65%
Texas	77%

Source: Dillman, 1978, pp. 22–25. The rates given there have been reduced by 10 percent to account for households not on sampling lists that could not be reached.

found on key questions, fears of sample bias can be laid to rest. If differences are found, data from the combined sample can be used if they are weighted for the differential sampling rates.

A less costly alternative that is often used is to compare the results of successive mailings. If no differences are found, it is assumed that the results would not change if efforts continued until most of those who did not cooperate with the first mailing responded. However, this method makes the strong and untested assumption that recipients who delay or forget to return a questionnaire until they are prompted to do so do not differ from those who consciously decide not to participate for one reason or another.

It is well known that recipients of mailed questionnaires who have strong positive or negative feelings about a topic or program are more likely to respond than recipients who are neutral. If the number of people who have strong positive feelings is roughly the same as the number of those who have strong negative feelings, the results will not be biased, but the strength of feeling will be overestimated. The results may be especially misleading if many people have little knowledge of a program and therefore do not respond.

Characteristics of Mailed Questionnaires

Eight major characteristics determine whether questionnaires can be mailed successfully: their length, the salience of their topic to potential respondents, the need to ask open-ended questions, the need to probe answers, the need for branching, possible order effects, the desirability or undesirability of allowing recipients to consult records or other people, and the recipient's need to absorb information.

Certain of these characteristics clearly point to the use of mailed questionnaires. Others argue for the use of personal interviews. In this section, we discuss these characteristics. Some are related to the possibility of obtaining sufficient cooperation from the sample, others to whether the respondents can understand and answer the questions without outside influences. There are many other aspects of questionnaire design that we will ignore, since they are common to all methods of administration.

Length of Questionnaire and Salience of Topics. It has long been known that mailed questionnaires must be shorter than personal interviews in order to obtain the same level of cooperation. This is because the respondents must make a greater effort and because there is no positive feedback from the interviewer. The obvious question is, How short is short? There is no single answer to this question. Two rules have been proposed: Six 8½ × 11 pages can be considered the maximum (Erdos and Morgan, 1970). There is little difference in the response rates for questionnaires of fewer than twelve pages and for questionnaires that contain fewer than 125 items for either the general public or specialized populations (Dillman, 1978).

These two rules are not really contradictory. Erdos and Morgan are referring to a typical market research survey about a product or service that a research firm conducts for an unnamed client. In this case, the salience to respondents is relatively low, and so the questionnaire must be fairly short. Dillman is referring mainly to surveys conducted by state agencies or universities in order to determine attitudes toward public policy issues. Such aims and sponsorship make the study more salient to respondents, in which case a twelve-page questionnaire becomes possible.

For special interest groups, particularly for professional groups whose members are highly educated or situations in which professional issues are the major concern, questionnaires of twenty pages or more are possible. That is, as the topic and the sponsorship increase in salience to respondents, so can the questionnaire become longer and still obtain a reasonable number of responses.

We must warn the reader that there is a strong tendency for policy evaluators to overestimate the knowledge and interest of respondents in the program being evaluated. Too long a questionnaire can very substantially reduce cooperation. It is always good practice to eliminate all questions that are not absolutely essential no matter how the data are to be gathered, but it is especially important to do so for mailed questionnaires.

Open-Ended Questions. This chapter is not the place for a discussion of the relative merits of closed and open-ended questions. Sudman and Bradburn (1982) have addressed that issue. Nevertheless, it is important to recognize that, if the questionnaire requires more than a few words of writing, it probably cannot be conducted by mail. Some kinds of open-ended questions can be asked by mail. These kinds include short-answer questions, such as the name of the cars or appliances that one owns, the prices that one has paid for goods, and where one was born or has lived. Respondents would not find it difficult or potentially embarrassing to answer these questions. However, questions that require a substantial amount of writing to answer, such as *What would you do to reduce crime in the United States?* or *What do you see as the major benefits (problems) of this program?* are likely to appear difficult, time-consuming, and potentially embarrassing. Many respondents will be concerned about making spelling and grammatical errors as well as about their ability to express themselves. The easiest way to avoid such difficulties is not to answer the questionnaire.

Questions that require a good deal of writing are also not appropriate for professional and other special groups. While the members of these groups may not be concerned about making errors or about expressing themselves, they will usually be concerned about the time that it takes to complete a questionnaire, and any open-ended question that requires substantial writing will be perceived as being too time-consuming. While we are generally sympathetic with fellow researchers, and we respond to almost all mail surveys that are sent to us, we invariably throw out any survey that starts with a request for a three- or four-page essay on the future of public opinion. However, we believe that it is courteous to leave space at the end of a questionnaire to enable any respondent who wishes to do so to make comments about any of the questions or to address topics that the questionnaire did not cover. Most respondents will not use this optional space, but those who do are more likely to respond to the rest of the questionnaire if they are given the opportunity to get something important off their chests.

Probing. In personal interviews, it is common for the interviewer to probe if the respondent's answer is incomplete or circular. This practice is impossible in mailed questionnaires. However, since probes are generally used after open-ended questions and since we have urged against the use of such questions on mailed questionnaires, this impossibility is no cause for regret.

Probes are also used to discover why someone did something or why someone has a favorable or negative attitude about a person or issue. If probing is deemed to be necessary, a subsample of respondents to a mailed questionnaire can be telephoned to obtain additional information. The subsample can be drawn from all respondents, or it can be limited to respondents who answer in specific ways.

Branching. By branching, we mean the process in which the answer to one question determines which alternative set of later questions the respondent is required to answer. Branching is fairly easy on all personal interviews, and it is particularly easy when computer-assisted telephone interviewing is used. Branching is extremely difficult on mailed questionnaires, and surveys that require complex branching cannot be conducted by mail. However, simple branching, such as omitting a question or questions that do not apply, is possible on mailed surveys. Dillman (1978) and Sudman and Bradburn (1982) discuss methods for formatting such questions.

However, even simple branches will sometimes be misunderstood by respondents to mailed questionnaires. The least harm is done if the respondent simply answers a question that should not have been answered, since that error can be corrected during the editing of the questionnaire. Confusion that leads respondents to omit questions that should have been answered is far more serious. Two kinds of complex branches are generally too difficult to use on mailed questionnaires: branches that depend on the answers to more than one question and sequential branches, that is, branches of branches.

If branching is too difficult for respondents, all is not lost. A policy evaluation questionnaire can be split into two parts—a brief screening questionnaire and a longer, substantive questionnaire. The brief screening questionnaire can be sent to all potential respondents, and when that questionnaire is returned, a second questionnaire can be sent that fits the special characteristics of the individual respondent. Determination of which second questionnaire to send can be made either by a computer or by hand in the central office. Although cooperation will drop off slightly, upwards of 90 percent of those who return the screening questionnaire will return the substantive questionnaire.

Order Effects. There is some possibility in all questionnaires that a respondent's answer will be affected by the answers that he or she gives to previous questions. Mailed questionnaires involve a special problem in this regard: A respondent's answers can be affected by questions that follow the given question. The typical respondent to a mailed questionnaire will read it through quickly to see what it contains before he or she answers any questions.

Funnel questions cannot be asked on mailed questionnaires. Funnel questions are used to determine the salience or importance of an issue. In a personal interview, a typical series of questions asked to determine concerns with air quality will proceed as follows:

1. What do you think is the most important problem facing this community today?
2. Here are a list of things that some people have mentioned as being problems in this community. Which do you think are serious problems:
   a. Crime
   b. Traffic
   c. Air pollution
3. How serious a problem is air pollution? Would you say it is very serious, serious, or not serious?

If the same sequence of questions were used in a mail survey, it would be obvious to potential respondents that the real topic was air quality, and questions 1 and 2 would be useless as measures of salience. Order effects also make it impossible to follow knowledge questions with attitude questions about a person, program, or policy, because the attitude questions provide clues that help respondents to answer the knowledge questions.

Consulting Records or Other People. In some program evaluation surveys, it may be highly desirable for respondents to consult records or talk with others in the household or organization. In this case, mailed surveys are preferable to personal interviews. The respondent in a personal interview always feels under pressure, and he or she will be reluctant to take time to search for documents. However, if unaided responses are desired, mail surveys are inappropriate. Even if the respondent is asked not to consult records or to talk with others, he or she will be tempted to do so, lest he or she appear ill informed. Thus, the same behavior—consulting records and other people—can be desirable or undesirable, depending on the purposes of the survey.

If the survey is attempting to measure behavior, it is desirable for respondents to consult records and other people. It is difficult to keep dates and details correct, especially if the events being discussed are frequent and of relatively low salience to respondents. Examining records, such as bills, receipts, cancelled checks, and even notes on a calendar, can help to reduce memory error. If respondents are reporting about the behavior of others within the household or the organization, the data that they provide will be more reliable than they would be if respondents were to rely on their own memory or incomplete knowledge.

However, if the survey is attempting to measure the attitudes of specified persons in households or organizations, mail methods can cause problems. There will be no problems if the person who receives the questionnaire has strong opinions about the questions asked or if all members of the group share the same views. However, if the recipient is not interested in the topic, while one or more other members of the same group are, the natural tendency is for the recipient either to consult with these others or to turn the questionnaire over to them to complete. As a result, there appears to be greater interest in the topic and more crystallized opinion than in fact exists.

Finally, if the survey is attempting to determine the respondents' knowledge about certain policies or issues, mailed questionnaires are inappropriate, even if they do not give hints on the correct answers. To avoid appearing ill informed, individual respondents may look up the information, ask other members of the group for the correct answer, or give the questionnaire to someone else to answer.

Need to Absorb Information. The use of mailed surveys to assess reaction to new products is widespread. In this application, the household is sent a new product that it is asked to use, or the product is described, and attitudes and behavioral intentions are obtained through mailed questionnaire. The same procedure can be used to assess reactions to a proposed program or policy. A description of the proposed program can be sent to respondents, who can then study the details before stating their attitudes. These descriptions must be simple and straightforward, since no one is available to explain complex details. However, the same rule applies to personal interviews. Interviewer explanations must be nonbiasing. Usually, they consist of a rereading of the same material. Mailed procedures have two advantages: Respondents can reread all or parts of the description as many times as necessary, and they have time to think about the alternatives. In a personal interview, the interviewer can feel pressure to finish the interview as rapidly as possible. The interviewer then puts subtle pressure on the respondent to answer questions without too much hesitation. In mail surveys, the respondent alone determines how much time to spend filling out the questionnaire. While a few respondents may rush through the questionnaire, those who want to think about their answers have the chance to do so.

Mailed questionnaires are the most convenient form for presenting visual material, such as pictures, lists, maps, and scales. Such material cannot be used in telephone interviews, but it can be handed to respondents in face-to-face interviews. Material that requires the operation of equipment, such as audio tapes or videotapes, films, and computers, and other complex products that require demonstration are inappropriate for mailed questionnaires.

Response Effects in Mailed Questionnaires

It will often be necessary to compare results obtained by a mailed questionnaire with results obtained by telephone or face-to-face interviews. It may also be necessary to combine the results of a mail survey with the results of personal interviews when the same question is asked by different methods. A key concern for program evaluators and others who wish to combine results from different data collection procedures is whether it is possible to do so. If the answers obtained by mail differ significantly from those obtained by other means, it is difficult to know what to do. Fortunately, method of administration appears to make little or no difference for a broad range of topics. While method effects can never be fully predicted without advance pilot tests, we summarize in this section what is known, referring readers who wish to know more to Sudman and Bradburn (1974) and to Bradburn and Sudman (1979). It is useful to differentiate threatening behavior questions, nonthreatening behavior questions, and attitude questions.

Nonthreatening Behavior Questions. It is difficult to define precisely what it meant by the terms *threatening questions* and *nonthreatening questions.* Threatening questions are those to which the respondent feels that society has a "right" answer. Thus, questions about voting behavior are threatening, because society expects one to vote. Similarly, questions about use of drugs or commission of crimes are threatening, because use of drugs and commission of crimes are illegal or contranormative. Nonthreatening questions are those for which there appears to be no right answer. Purchases of groceries or clothing or a visit to the dentist within the past two weeks are nonthreatening for almost all respondents. However, it must be recognized that even the most threatening question will not be threatening to all respondents, while even innocuous questions may be threatening to a few.

Experience indicates that nonthreatening questions are not affected by the method of administration. This does not mean that the answers to such questions are always correct. Nonthreatening behavior questions can be subject to large memory errors, and behavior can be overstated or understated, depending on the amount of time involved. There may also be errors in details. These errors are independent of the method of administration (Cannell and Fowler, 1963; Hochstim, 1967; Sudman and Bradburn, 1974; Bradburn and Sudman, 1979).

Socially Desirable Behavior. Respondents tend to overreport socially desirable behavior, such as voting, charitable giving, and participation in cultural activities (Sudman and Bradburn, 1974). Here, small differences have been observed between responses obtained by mail and personal methods. The levels of overreporting are generally slightly lower on mail surveys than they are in personal interviews, as Table 3 shows. Most researchers believe that mail is superior to personal interviewing methods in this respect, because

Table 3. Levels of Over- or Underreporting for Self-Administered Questionnaires and Personal Interviews

	Percent Over- or Underreporting	
	Self-Administered Questionnaires	Personal Interviews
Socially Desirable		
Own a library card	18%	20%
Registered to vote	12%	16%
Voted in primary	36%	35%
Socially Undesirable		
Declared bankruptcy	− 32%	− 36%
Arrested for drunken driving	− 54%	− 46%

respondents have less need to report socially desirable behavior to an unknown researcher than they do to an interviewer with whom they are interacting.

If only one method of administration is to be used, the more valid results will come from the mailed questionnaire. If a combination of procedures is contemplated, the researcher will face a problem. It is not possible simply to combine the results of the two procedures without taking their differential levels of reporting accuracy into account, nor is it possible to estimate those different levels of accuracy unless a randomized experiment has been conducted. In the normal situation, where a mailed questionnaire is followed up by telephone interviews with a subsample of those who did not respond, sample characteristic effects and response effects cannot be separated. One solution in this case is to use adjustments based on data from previous work if they exist; another is to do some small experiments to measure response differences.

The magnitude of the differences by method depends on the level of threat and on the proportion of respondents who have not engaged in the activity. Thus, the likelihood of method differences seems to be greatest for moderately threatening questions. If most people have engaged in the behavior or if the level of threat is low, as it is on a question like *Do you have a public library card?*, then the researcher may be willing to ignore the usually small differences between mail and personal methods.

Socially Undesirable Behavior. While the reader might think that the results for socially undesirable behavior would be identical to the results for socially desirable behavior, the differences prove to be more complex. For very threatening questions, the preponderance of evidence suggests that there are no significant differences by method. Even though mail procedures are less personal than interview procedures, it appears that respondents are unwilling to report having committed socially undesirable acts, even if the questionnaire appears to guarantee anonymity. Many respondents feel that there is some way of identifying the person who filled out the questionnaire, even if no name is requested.

Table 3 summarizes some findings comparing results from personal interviews and self-administered questionnaires for socially undesirable behavior. Table 3 clearly indicates that very undesirable behavior is significantly underreported, regardless of method. We will not discuss such procedures as randomized response and alternative question wordings that have been used to reduce such errors. The interested reader can find a discussion in Bradburn and Sudman (1979).

For behaviors that are moderately socially undesirable, self-administered questionnaires produce higher levels of reported behavior than personal interviews do. Thus, Thorndike and others (1952) found that respondents to a self-administered form reported approximately 15 percent more psychosomatic symptoms than did respondents in face-to-face interviews. The largest difference was on the question *Have you frequently suffered from constipation?* Sixteen percent of the respondents said yes on the self-administered form, while only 8 percent of those interviewed did. Hochstim (1967) found that more women reported discussing female medical problems and Papanicolaou tests with their husbands on self-administered questionnaires than they did in telephone and face-to-face interviews. However, no differences were found by method on questions related to the drinking of beer, wine, and liquor. These results are summarized in Table 4.

Attitude Questions. Just as methods sometimes produce response differences on behavioral questions, they can also lead to differences on attitudinal questions. However, these differences occur only on a small minority of questions, where social norms indicate what the correct answer should be.

Table 4. Comparisons of Women's Responses to Health Questions by Self-Administered Questionnaires and Personal Interviews

Item	Percent	
	Self-Administered Questionnire (N = 507)	*Personal Interview (N = 439)*
Discuss female medical problems with husband	68%	50%
Discuss Papanicolaou test	40%	31%
Drink beer	49%	47%
Drink wine	54%	52%
Drink whiskey or liquor	64%	61%

Source: Hochstim, 1967.

Such situations are reflected in Table 5, which presents differences between self-administered questionnaires and personal interviews on a series of questions dealing with various aspects of religious behavior (Sudman, 1967). Catholic respondents were much more candid on the self-administered form, while their answers were similar to those of Protestants in the personal interview, presumably because Protestants set the norms. These differences are typical. Where differences exist, self-administered questionnaires almost always provide the most candid reports of attitudes.

Mailed questionnaires can also be preferred to personal interviews in situations where the interviewer's characteristics are related to the survey topic and thus have an effect on responses. This can occur if the survey topic is racial or sexual attitudes. The respondent can see the race and sex of the interviewer, and some respondents will give an answer that they presume to be socially acceptable to the interviewer. Thus, those who have studied racial attitudes have noted that whites are more positive about black rights and that blacks are more militant in demanding their rights if the interviewer is black. Similarly, men will report more negative attitudes toward rape if the interviewer is female.

There is also the possibility that interviewers will mishear or miscode a response based either on their preconceptions or on random error. In our experience, this is not a very serious problem. It should also be remembered that experienced interviewers probably make fewer coding errors than do the respondents to mailed questionnaires.

Mailed questionnaires are generally to be preferred when method produces differences in attitudes. However, most of the time it does not. In the study whose results are displayed in Table 5, differences of 5 percent or more were found only on the thirteen statements shown there. For the remaining thirty-one statements, the differences were too small to be consequential. Since this volume is addressed to program evaluators, the reader may wonder whether method can create differences for questions that deal with satisfaction about an agency or a service received. Are recipients more candid in a mail survey than they are in personal interviews? The evidence suggests that the answer is no if the personal interviews are conducted in the home. However, there is some evidence, as we have already noted, that responses will be positively biased toward the agency if the questionnaires are handed to respondents in person or if respondents complete the questionnaires while they are at the agency to receive some service.

Summary

This brief review of the possible response effects of mailed questionnaires and personal interviews clearly favors the use of mailed questionnaires if the general limitations of mail surveys are not serious in the particular case. For most questions, particularly for questions related to program evaluation,

Table 5. Agreement with Statements in Catholic and Protestant Personal Interviews and Catholic Self-Administered Questionnaires

Statement	Percentage Agreeing		
	Catholics: Personal Interviews	Catholics: Self-Administered Questionnaires	Protestants: Personal Interviews
Personal answers more socially acceptable (differences larger than 4 percent):			
Taken altogether, how would you say things are these days — would you say that you are very happy ?	36%	23%	40%
Even though a person has a hard time making ends meet, he should still try to give some of his money to help the poor.	81	74	76
God doesn't really care how He is worshipped so long as He is worshipped.	72	62	69
Negroes shouldn't push themselves where they are not wanted.	60	68	62
Have you spent any time by yourself in the past few months helping someone who needs help?	64	52	57
A good man can earn heaven by his own efforts alone.	65	58	53
The United States should do more to help the poorer nations by building hospitals, schools, and homes in these places.	70	63	65
I would strongly disapprove if a Negro family moved next door to me.	37	43	40
A student should be free to make up his own mind on what he learns in school.	59	54	60
Two people who are in love do not do anything wrong when they marry, even though one of them has been divorced.	52	47	87
Personal answers less socially acceptable (differences larger than 4 percent):			
It would be wrong to take considerable time off while working for a large company, even though the company would not be hurt by it at all.	50	66	55
It is all right to refuse to talk to some member of the family after a disagreement, especially if the argument was the fault of the other.	27	20	25
Rules should never be relaxed, because children will take advantage of it.	65	60	61

method produces no differences. When differences do exist, it is usually the case that the more accurate responses come from the self-administered mailed questionnaires.

Serious concern about method differences should arise only when three conditions are present: Both mail and personal interviewing procedures are used, a behavior or attitude question with a socially correct answer is asked or the interviewer's characteristics are related to the topic of the study, and the question is only moderately threatening. For very threatening questions, the differences created by method of administration are swamped by the under-reporting that the threat itself causes.

References

Bradburn, N. M., Sudman, S., and Associates. *Improving Interview Method and Question-naire Design: Response Effects to Threatening Questions in Survey Research.* San Francisco: Jossey-Bass, 1979.

Cannell, C. F., and Fowler, F. J. "A Comparison of a Self-Enumerative Procedure and a Personal Interview: A Validity Study." *Public Opinion Quarterly,* 1963, *27,* 250–264.

Dillman, D. *Mail and Telephone Surveys: The Total Design Method.* New York: Wiley-Interscience, 1978.

Erdos, P. L., and Morgan, A. J. *Professional Mail Surveys.* New York: McGraw-Hill, 1970.

Hochstim, J. R. "A Critical Comparison of Three Strategies of Collecting Data from Households." *Journal of the American Statistical Association,* 1967, *62,* 976–989.

Sudman, S. *Reducing the Cost of Surveys.* Chicago: Aldine, 1967.

Sudman, S., and Bradburn, N. M. *Response Effects in Surveys: A Review and Synthesis.* Chicago: Aldine, 1974.

Sudman, S., and Bradburn, N. M. *Asking Questions: A Practical Guide to Questionnaire Design.* San Francisco: Jossey-Bass, 1982.

Thorndike, R. L., Hagen, E., and Kemper, R. A. "Normative Data Obtained in the House-to-House Administration of a Psychosomatic Inventory." *Journal of Consulting Psychology,* 1952, *16,* 257–260.

Seymour Sudman is director of NORC at the University of Chicago.

Norman Bradburn is professor of business administration and sociology at the University of Illinois, Champaign-Urbana.

The empirical effects of adherence to details of the Total Design Method approach to the design of mail surveys is discussed.

The Importance of Adhering to Details of the Total Design Method (TDM) for Mail Surveys

Don A. Dillman
Joye J. Dillman
Carole J. Makela

Since its publication in 1978, the Total Design Method (TDM) has been used extensively to conduct mail surveys. It has been shown capable of consistently producing response rates above 60 percent in samples of the general public (Dillman, 1978). One likely reason for the extensive use of the TDM is the prescription of virtually all details involved in conducting mail surveys, from size of stationery to number and timing of follow-ups. The prescriptive detail of the TDM is also disconcerting, for two reasons. First, certain details are more difficult for some researchers to use than are others, leading to the desire to substitute procedures. Secondly, and even more disconcerting, no evidence exists on the importance of many specific details of the TDM to achieving the highest possible response rates. The question facing many researchers is which and how many deviations from the prescribed TDM will significantly affect response rates.

The research on which the chapter is based was sponsored by the Agricultural Experiment Station in eleven states under Western Region Project W159.

D. C. Lockhart (Ed.). *Making Effective Use of Mailed Questionnaires.*
New Directions for Program Evaluation, no. 21. San Francisco: Jossey-Bass, March 1984.   **49**

It is most unlikely that experiments will be conducted to determine the importance of every detail of the TDM. To do so would require a large number of experiments in which the effect of each individual detail was tested. Inasmuch as the effects of some aspects of the TDM (for instance, personalization) may be greater under low response conditions (that is, no follow-ups) than when the full TDM is used, it is not enough to simultaneously vary all details in a very large factorial design (which in itself would be difficult to do). Instead, multiple experiments need to be done in which the control group receives the full TDM treatment, except for the procedure being tested.

A further difficulty in conducting such experiments is that large sample sizes are needed (Dillman, 1978). It is unlikely that the response rate effects of some aspects of the TDM will be as much as a full percentage point under the high response rate conditions of the TDM, where each additional percent of response becomes more difficult to achieve.

Pressures to deviate from the TDM are considerable. Many researchers are unable to access the prescribed size and weight of paper or the recommended printing equipment. Others feel it is necessary to cut labor-intensive activities such as individually signed letters and postcards. Because of costs, mail surveys are often the only survey alternative for some people. Thus, it is not surprising that further efforts to cut costs of mail surveys are frequently sought.

Implementation of a common survey in eleven states provided an opportunity to examine the difficulties of researchers in precisely replicating the TDM procedures (Makela and others, 1982). This survey also provided some insight into the necessity of the full use of the prescribed procedures. The research reported here is a case study and not a controlled experiment. Although identical questionnaires were administered in eleven states to similarly drawn samples of the general public, the fact that each survey was conducted in a different state by a different university may in itself account for response rate differences. However, if elimination or alteration of certain aspects of the TDM is found to correlate with lower response, the results will raise questions about the omitted or altered aspects of the TDM, providing justification and direction for the future pursuit of carefully designed experiments.

An added benefit of this study stems from the fact that the researchers responsible for the individual state surveys had agreed in principle to use the same procedures in all states. Thus, where deviations occurred, they were, for the most part, ones the investigators felt forced to make because of the limitations of resources. These deviations from the TDM are ones that other researchers will be tempted to use and for which data are therefore needed about the likely results.

Finally, this chapter provides insight into some of the difficulties involved in realizing certain potentials of the mail survey, that is surveying large samples of the general public with large enough numbers of cases from geographic subregions or population subgroups to allow detailed comparisons. The sample size for the study on which this article is based was 17,213 households.

The Study

The surveys were conducted by researchers in the agricultural experiment stations of ten western states (Arizona, California, Colorado, Idaho, Montana, Nevada, Oregon, Utah, Washington and Wyoming) and one eastern state (Pennsylvania) (Makela and others, 1982). Done under the rubric of the USDA research system the researchers from each of the participating land-grant universities agreed to implement the same questionnaire to a minimum of 1500 respondents in their states following an updated version of the TDM. Sample frames for all states except Pennsylvania consisted of current telephone directories. Directories were stratified by metropolitan counties (urban) and nonmetropolitan counties (rural). Simple random samples of equal size were drawn from each strata. In Pennsylvania, names were sampled from driver's license lists.

The questionnaire concerned household energy issues and included ten pages of questions. These questions ranged from general attitudes about U.S. energy policy and energy saving actions taken by the household to the amount of fuels consumed and demographics such as education and income. Following TDM procedures, the questionnaire was printed in booklet form with an attractive front cover and a back cover that solicited additional comments.

The surveys in nine states were implemented beginning March 9, 1981. The two remaining states began implementation within a month of that date.

Cover letters had the same content in every state. The questionnaire and cover letter used in the study were approved by Human Subjects Protection Committees of the respective universities. Thus, in addition to the usual message of why the respondent was important and the social usefulness of the study, potential respondents were informed that their participation in the study was voluntary. Accordingly, they were asked to return the questionnaire blank if they preferred not to participate. Two versions of the cover letter were used. One letter requested completion by an adult male and the other asked for completion by an adult female. Each version was systematically assigned in an alternating fashion to households in both the rural and urban strata.

Letters were individually typed on Monarch size stationery ($10\frac{1}{2}" \times 7\frac{1}{4}"$) for mailing in appropriate envelopes $10\frac{3}{4}" \times 7\frac{1}{2}"$). Individual names and addresses were typed at the top of the letters and because of subject selection, no salutations were used. The mailout date was included on the letter, and each letter was individually signed with a blue ballpoint pen. The questionnaire had an identification number stamped in plain view on the front for purposes of follow-up. A stamped return envelope was included with the mailing. The individually addressed envelopes were mailed first class.

One week after the original mailing, postcards were sent to all households. The postcards were designed as a thank you and reminder and the same message was used in all states. The postcard included a mailout date and the investigator's signature applied with a blue ballpoint pen. The name and address for the household was applied individually, rather than by means of a label.

Three weeks after the original mailout a replacement questionnaire was sent using the same procedures as in the first mailing but including a somewhat different cover letter. No distinction was made between male and female in this mailing. Two alternatives were prescribed for the third follow-up. One possibility was a telephone follow-up designed as a friendly call to answer questions the nonrespondents might have; this was scheduled to occur several days after the second follow-up. The other was a second replacement questionnaire sent by special delivery or certified mail.

The TDM implementation procedures published in Dillman (1978) were modified to take advantage of advances in equipment and subsequent findings on improving TDM response rates. First, where available, word processing equipment was used to type each letter (instead of multilithing the body and adding an inside address). Second, stamped return (rather than business reply) envelopes were used. This was done because stamped returns had been shown in four previous TDM experiments to have an advantage of at least two percentage points in response rate (Dillman and Moore, 1983). Finally, the alternative final follow-ups were allowed because previous experiments had shown very little difference in effect and it was unclear which procedure was superior (Dillman and Moore, 1983). In addition, some investigators were interested in experimenting with the alternatives as part of the final follow-up.

Individual State Modification

Considerable variation existed in the extent to which the individual states adhered to prescribed TDM procedures. Some states made virtually no deviations, others made a substantial number.

Arizona. There were two deviations from the TDM. First, a mailout date was omitted from the postcard follow-up, contributing to a less personalized appearance. More significantly, a telephone call was substituted for the third follow-up but it was not implemented until three weeks after the second follow-up.

California. A number of deviations from the TDM were made, more than in any of the other states. First, the letters were printed by computer and photocopied onto letterhead stationery. Although the type was obviously printed by a computer, we judged it to have a personalized appearance. Second, ordinary business-size stationery was used instead of the Monarch-size. Third, address labels were used on all envelopes. Fourth, a business reply envelope was used instead of a stamped return envelope. Fifth, a postcard follow-up contained no mailout date, and the project leader's signature was multilithed in black as was the message. Sixth, address labels were used on the postcards. Seventh, the third contact was similar to the first contact. Eighth, the third follow-up was different from that used in any other state, consisting of a postcard very similar in content to the postcard follow-up previously used. No further efforts to contact nonresponding households were made.

Colorado. Only one deviation from the TDM was made in this state. The postcard follow-up did not include a date and the signature was pre-printed in black. At the time of the third follow-up, the nonresponding house-holds were divided into two groups. Eighty percent were sent a certified letter that included a replacement questionnaire. This letter was prepared in much the same fashion as the preceding two letters. The remainder received a telephone call. However, those not contacted by telephone after several attempts received no further mailings.

Idaho. The second follow-up in this state used a form letter that con-tained no inside address. It did include an individually applied blue ballpoint signature. All subjects who had not responded by the time for the third follow-up were called, similar to the procedure used in Arizona. No follow-up mail-ing was sent to those who could not be reached by telephone.

Montana. Several deviations of a somewhat different nature were made in this state. First, the initial cover letter was multilithed on ordinary business size stationery. Individual addresses were applied in an effort to match the type. Postcards with address labels were sent only to households that did not respond to the first mailing. The third contact was a form letter with the salutation "To a very important person" in place of the inside name and ad-dress. Efforts were made to contact some nonrespondents by telephone but these efforts were terminated before all could be contacted because of the cost. No further efforts to contact respondents were made.

Nevada. Regular university letterhead stationery instead of Monarch was used for all mailings. On the postcard follow-up, a preprinted black signa-ture was used. Similar to Montana, a form letter was used for the second follow-up using the salutation "To a very important person" in place of the in-side name and address. One month after the second follow-up, nonrespon-dents were telephoned. Only one attempt was made to contact the household. There were no further efforts to contact nonrespondents.

Oregon. There were two deviations from the TDM. A multilith letter which contained no inside address or salutation was used for the third contact. No third follow-up of any kind was made.

Utah. Multilith cover letters were used, but there existed considerable contrast between the printing and the typed-in name and address. Each letter was signed with a fine black pen that gave the appearance of a preprinted sig-nature. The postcard follow-up was not dated, but did contain the individually applied blue ballpoint pen signature. The second follow-up was a form letter with the general salutation "To a very important person" in place of the inside address. A blue preprinted signature was used. No third follow-up of any kind was made.

Washington. The full TDM was used in this state. However, households that had not responded by the time of the third contact were divided alternately into two groups. One group received a telephone call between three and ten days after the third contact. Those households which could not be contacted after a minimum of four attempts were sent a special delivery letter, as was done for the other test group. This second group was sent letters (on regular size letterhead) and replacement questionnaires in much the same fashion as the other mailings except that they were sent by special delivery mail.

Wyoming. A multilith letter with name and address inserted was used in the first mailing. A similar letter was used in the third contact. All households not responding by the time of the fourth contact were called. Households not reached by telephone did not receive another mail contact.

Pennsylvania. All letters used in Pennsylvania were preprinted and had inside names and addresses added in matching type. The signature on all letters was preprinted in blue. A high quality print job gave the letters the appearance of being personalized. The postcard follow-up contained no mailout date and the signature was preprinted in blue. At the time of the third contact, the remaining households were divided into three groups. One group received a telephone contact shortly after the third follow-up and those who could not be reached were included in the second treatment group, which received a fourth mailing sent by special delivery. The letter looked much like previous letters. A third group was treated similarly to the second group except that the letter was sent by certified mail.

Results

In order to compare the extent of adherence to TDM implementation procedures among the various states, we first identified those procedures not followed by one or more states. Those procedures are listed in Table 1.

Each state is identified in this table according to whether it wholly or partly utilized the prescribed TDM procedure. A "1" indicates the TDM procedure was wholly utilized by a state and a "½" indicates the procedure was partly followed. A "0" indicates the procedure was not used at all. Fractions identify procedures fully used on equivalent portions (¼ or ½) of a sample, because of the methodological experiments being conducted.

Substantial variations among the states are revealed in this table. The most significant variation in the first mailout is the use by five of the states of multilith letters instead of individually typed letters. Three states chose to use regular size stationery and two used altered signature methods.

Deviations from the postcard follow-up primarily consisted of the lack of inclusion of a date and individually applied signatures, both of which tended to depersonalize this mailing. Six states did not follow the prescribed procedures in one or both of these areas.

A substantial amount of deviation occurred at the time of the second follow-up when three states switched to form letters without including names and addresses. However, the most significant departures occurred in the third follow-up. Two states — Utah and Oregon — made no third follow-up. One state — California — substituted a postcard follow-up so that no replacement questionnaire was provided. Three other states — Nevada, Arizona, and Idaho — made telephone calls, but they did so in different ways. Montana made telephone calls to only some of the households and followed the telephone call with a replacement questionnaire if requested. In Nevada only one attempt was made to call households before terminating all efforts to reach them. In Arizona, several attempts were made and a questionnaire was remailed if requested.

Four states implemented the recommended procedures of two or more attempts at telephoning with those calls occurring shortly after the second follow-up had been sent. In two of these states — Washington and Pennsylvania — households not contacted after several attempts received another letter and replacement questionnaire. However, in Colorado and Wyoming, no further contact with these households was made. Finally, in three of the above-mentioned states telephone calls were made only to a portion of the households. The remainder of each sample was treated experimentally and received a follow-up questionnaire by either certified or special delivery mail. The specifics of these final mailings are detailed in Table 1.

There is no unequivocal way to summarize the overall extent to which each state followed the prescribed TDM procedures. Some elements on which there was variation among states, for instance, whether a third follow-up was made, are undoubtedly more important to response than others, for instance, whether the follow-up postcard was dated. At the same time, there are no criteria available for differentially weighting each of the TDM procedures. Consequently it was arbitrarily decided to score one point for having done each procedure, one-half point for having partially done a procedure or completing it in a somewhat different way, and no points for not having done it at all. States that experimented with the telephone and mail alternatives for the third follow-up were given half credit for each procedure used in these follow-ups so as not to provide credit simply for having done both types of follow-up.

Scores on this index of adherence to the TDM ranged from 6½ for California to 21½ for Washington, with a mean of 15.1 and a s.d of 4.26. Thus, there is considerable variation in the extent to which the TDM principles were followed in implementing the study.

Disposition of Questionnaires

Sample sizes deviated somewhat from the prescribed 1,500, ranging from 1,409 in Utah to 2,166 in Pennsylvania, for a total of 17,213 households. The response rate (number of usable returned questionnaires divided by number mailed) was 59.0 percent, ranging from 38.0 percent in California to

Table 1. Adherence to Prescribed TDM Procedures by Each State

Recommended TDM Procedures	Arizona	California	Colorado	Idaho	Montana	Nevada	Oregon	Pennsylvania	Utah	Washington	Wyoming
First Mailout											
Original typed letters	1	½	1	1	½	1	1	½	½	1	½
Inside address added	1	1	1	1	1	1	1	1	1	1	1
Monarch instead of regular size stationery	1	0	1	1	0	0	1	1	1	1	1
Blue ballpoint signature (vs. preprinted)	1	1	1	1	1	1	1	½	0	1	1
Address typed onto envelopes	1	0	1	1	1	1	1	1	1	1	1
Stamped return envelope (instead of business reply)	1	0	1	1	1	1	1	1	1	1	1
Postcard Follow-up											
Sent one week after first mailout	1	1	1	1	1	1	1	1	1	1	1
Contained mailout date	0	0	0	1	1	1	1	0	0	1	1
Blue ballpoint signature	1	0	0	1	1	0	1	½	1	1	1
Address typed onto card (instead of label)	1	0	1	1	½	1	1	1	1	1	1
Second Follow-up											
Original typed letters	1	½	1	0	0	0	0	½	0	1	½
Inside address added	1	1	1	0	0	0	0	1	0	1	1
Monarch stationery	1	0	1	1	0	0	1	1	1	1	1
Blue ballpoint signature	1	1	1	1	1	1	1	½	½	1	1
Address typed onto envelope	1	0	1	1	1	1	1	1	1	1	1
Stamped return envelope	1	0	1	1	1	1	1	1	1	1	1

Third Follow-up											
Telephone, within 1–2 weeks of third contact	½	1	½*	½	½	½	0	½*	0	½*	1
Mail contact four weeks after third	0	½*	½	0	0	0	0	½*	0	½*	0
If telephone											
Questionnaire remailed if requested	1	0	½*	1	½	0	0	½*	0	½*	1
2 + attempts to contact	1	0	½*	1	½	0	0	½*	0	½*	1
Households not contacted; sent questionnaire by mail	0	0	0	0	0	0	0	½*	0	½*	0
If mail											
Original typed letter	0	0	½*	0	0	0	0	¼**	0	½*	0
Inside address added	0	0	½*	0	0	0	0	½*	0	½*	0
Monarch stationery	0	0	½*	0	0	0	0	½*	0	0	0
Blue ballpoint signature	0	0	½*	0	0	0	0	¼**	0	½*	0
Address typed onto envelope	0	0	½*	0	0	0	0	½*	0	½*	0
Stamped return envelope	0	0	½*	0	0	0	0	½*	0	½*	0
Certified postage	0	0	½	0	0	0	0	½*	0	½*	0
Special delivery postage	0	0	0	0	0	0	0	¼*	0	½*	0
Index of Adherence to TDM Procedures	17½	6½	19½	16½	12½	11½	14	18½	11	21½	18

Note: 1 means procedure was used (1 point), ½ means procedure was partially used (½ point), and 0 means procedure was not used (0 points). Those fractions with asterisks (¼ and ½) mean procedure was fully used on part of the sample due to application of an experiment. Fractions with double asterisks mean technique was partially used on half of sample.

cent in Washington. Returned questionnaires less than 70 pecent complete were considered refusals. Complete disposition of the questionnaires by state and strata is presented in Table 2.

No generalization can be made about differences in urban-rural response rates, a factor that might be looked to in order to explain differences in response among states. Response rates for urban (metropolitan counties) were somewhat higher in Arizona, California, Colorado, Idaho, Utah, and Washington than for the corresponding rural areas. However, rural response rates were higher in Nevada, Oregon, Wyoming, and Pennsylvania. The mean response rates for urban and rural regions were virtually the same.

Information on the number of households that received a questionnaire but did not return a completed one provides another perspective for examining the effectiveness of TDM procedures. Effectiveness can be analyzed in two ways. First, if the questionnaire does not reach an eligible household, none of the response-inducing technques have an opportunity to influence the householder. Therefore, the proportion of households reached but which did not respond provides an inverse indicator of the effectiveness of the survey procedures. The higher the number of households not heard from by the end of the survey, the less effective the procedures can be considered to be. Second, a related indicator of effectiveness can be constructed by combining the number of households registering an overt refusal with the number of households left outstanding. The most effective mail survey procedures should minimize both of these variables. An additional reason for combining them is that use of the telephone as a final follow-up tends to increase the number of overt refusals and decrease the number of households not heard from.

Table 2 reveals that the percent never heard from ranges from 17.2 percent for Colorado to 37.6 percent for California with a mean of 24.1. The percent never heard from plus overt refusals ranged from 25.8 percent in Washington to 50.4 percent in California. Thus, considerable variation exists in both of these measures of TDM effectiveness. Proportion of households not heard from in California was more than doubled than that for Colorado.

Comparisons

Table 3 ranks the states from highest to lowest in terms of adherence to the prescribed TDM procedures. It is apparent that there is a substantial, albeit imperfect, correlation between the index of adherence to TDM procedures and the overall response rate. For example, two of the three highest three states on the index — Washington, Colorado, and Pennsylvania, in that order — are similarly ranked on response rates. Two of the three lowest on the index — Nevada and California — are also lowest on response rates. But, Utah, which is next to last (tenth) on the index is fourth on response rates. A Spearman rank-difference correlation coefficient (rho) of .81 exists for the association between ranking (Table 4).

Table 2. Questionnaire Disposition, by State

Sample Component	Arizona	California	Colorado	Idaho	Montana[a]	Nevada	Oregon	Utah	Washington	Wyoming	Pennsylvania	Total
Questionnaires mailed	1,498	1,655	1,480	1,500	1,500	1,501	1,503	1,409	1,501	1,500	2,166	17,213
Questionnaire disposition												
Usable returns												
Rural	423	258	452	395	436	413	423	451	484	446	702	4,883
Urban	424	370	487	437	459	322	410	377	489	436	631	4,842
Unidentified	2	1	11	2	13	2	1	2	4	0	0	38
Total	849	629	950	834	908	737	834	830	977	882	1,333	9,763
Not delivered	114	337	111	118		250	137	78	142	236	62	1,585
Ineligible respondents (dead, moved, in nursing home, no English, etc.)	46	25	33	25		15	24	20	32	30	25	275
Total	160	362	144	143		265	161	98	174	266	87	1,860
Overt refusals	212	169	150	210		225	101	30	98	120	313	1,628
Never heard from	277	495	236	313		274	407	451	252	232	433	3,370
Total	1,498	1,655	1,480	1,500		1,501	1,503	1,409	1,501	1,500	2,166	15,713
Response rate (Percent usable of total mailed)												
Rural	56.0	34.2	60.7	52.7		54.6	56.2	58.0	64.5	59.5	64.8	56.6
Urban	57.1	41.1	66.3	58.3		43.3	54.7	59.7	65.2	58.1	58.3	56.4
Total	56.7	38.0	64.2	55.6	60.5	49.1	55.5	58.9	65.1	58.8	63.5	57.0

Table 2. Questionnaire Disposition, by State (*continued*)

Sample Component	Arizona	California	Colorado	Idaho	Montana[a]	Nevada	Oregon	Utah	Washington	Wyoming	Pennsylvania	Total
Completion rate (Usable returns as percent number mailed less undelivered and ineligible)	63.5	48.6	61.1	61.5		59.6	62.1	63.3	73.6	71.5	64.1	63.6
Percent never heard from (as percent of number delivered)	20.0	37.6	17.2	22.7		21.9	29.8	33.9	18.5	18.4	20.6	24.1
Percent never heard from plus overt refusals (as percent of number delivered)	35.5	50.4	28.2	37.8		39.9	37.2	36.1	25.8	27.9	35.5	35.4

[a]Complete data on disposition of questionnaires not available.

Table 3. Comparison of Adherence to TDM Index,
Response Rate, and Percent not Heard from by State

State	Adherence to TDM		Response Rate (Percent of total mailed)		Not Heard from		Not Heard from plus Overt Refusals	
	Index	Rank[a]	Percent	Rank	Percent	Rank	Percent	Rank
Washington	21.5	1	65.1	1	18.5	3	25.8	1
Colorado	20.5	2	64.2	2	17.2	1	28.2	3
Pennsylvania	18.0	3.5	61.5	3	20.6	5	35.5	5
Wyoming	18.0	3.5	58.8	5	18.4	2	27.9	2
Arizona	17.5	5	56.7	6	20.0	4	35.3	4
Idaho	16.5	6	55.6	7	22.7	7	37.8	8
Oregon	14.0	7	55.5	8	29.8	8	37.2	7
Montana	12.5		60.5					
Nevada	11.5	8	49.1	9	21.9	6	39.9	9
Utah	11.0	9	58.9	4	33.9	9	36.1	6
California	6.5	10	38.0	10	37.6	10	50.4	10

[a]Montana is not ranked due to missing data.

62

Table 4. Spearman Rank-Difference Correlations for Adherence to TDM Index and Three Measures of Effectiveness of Mail Survey Procedures

Measures Correlated with Index of Adherence to TDM	r	r²	z	p
Response rate[a]	.81	65.6	2.43	.0075
Percent not heard from	.90	81.0	2.70	.0035
Percent not heard from plus overt refusals	.88	77.4	2.63	.0043

[a]If Montana is included, $r = .71$; $r^2 = 50.4$, $z = 2.25$; $p = .0122$.

Comparisons of the adherence to TDM index to proportion of households not heard from (expressed as a percent of those to which the questionnaire was delivered) reveals much similarity to the above results; the Spearman rho for this comparison is .90. The top five states are the same in both rankings. In these five states—Washington, Colorado, Pennsylvania, Wyoming, and Arizona—responses of some type were elicited from four-fifths or more of the households to which questionnaires were delivered. A possible reason for the low ranking of Utah on the index, but not on response rates emerges from this comparison. Utah is second from the bottom (the higher the proportion, the lower the rank) on proportion of respondents not heard from. Significantly, Utah, which did not use a third follow-up, had more respondents not heard from than any other state except California, which used substantially fewer TDM procedures than any other state.

Expanding the group of those not heard from to include overt refusals results in a ranking only slightly different from the previous ranking (Table 3). The big change in ranking is for Utah, which changes from ninth to sixth. The correlation with the adherence to TDM index rank remains about the same, at .88 (Table 4.).

Discussion and Conclusions

The major concern addressed in this chapter is whether the lack of adherence to details of the TDM results in lower response rates. Differences among the eleven states in the extent to which prescribed details were followed was the result of decisions of individual investigators and not of random assignment. This limited our ability to attribute lower response rates only to the omission of certain procedures. Furthermore, each state constitutes a discrete subpopulation of the general public and each university a separate entity for survey administration. These factors may also be responsible for differences in response rate. We cannot judge the extent to which these factors might be responsible for the response rate differences reported here. Our conclusions must therefore be somewhat limited and focus on possible reasons for having foregone certain procedures and implications of the findings for future experimentation. The TDM procedures altered tended to be those that required equipment to which researchers had difficulty getting access — word processing equipment or labor intensive activities such as individually putting inside addresses onto preprinted letters. There was general compliance with basic decision issues such as timing of follow-ups and use of stamped returns (instead of business reply envelopes).

The biggest variation by far was at the time of the third follow-up. Eight distinct sets of third follow-up procedures were used in the eleven states, ranging from none at all in two states to full implementation of the prescribed TDM procedures in two others. Interviews with each of the researchers suggested that three factors influenced the substantial modification of procedures at this point, all of which tended to reinforce one another. One reason was that the amount of effort and resources required to conduct the previous three mailings were somewhat greater than the researchers had expected. The fourth contact, either by telephone or special mail, would have been by far the most costly. Second, some researchers felt they had already achieved a reasonably good response rate and did not feel compelled to push it higher. Finally, because of considerable communication among researchers during the implementation stage, there was a general awareness that some researchers were considering changing procedures for the third follow-up and that others saw it as an acceptable and easier path to follow.

One implication of this experience is that the later stages of the TDM seem particularly sensitive to being foregone. Thus, research that proves or disproves the need for adherence in later stages seems an important focus for future work. For most researchers, the first mailing and postcard follow-up can be easily done; it is the second and third follow-ups that test patience and perseverance.

The relationship between adherence to TDM procedures and response rates is in the direction of suggesting that greater adherence results in higher response. The three highest ranking states and two of the three lowest ranking states on the adherence to TDM index were identically ranked for response rates. The case for the existence of a strong relationship is strengthened by a consideration of proportion of households that received questionnaires and were not heard from. States that did not use the third follow-up left an exceptionally high proportion of households in the not heard from category. There is little doubt that their response rate could have been significantly improved by adherence to that TDM procedure. It is also significant that none of the states using a form letter second follow-up were in the top five in proportion of households not heard from (lower proportion ranks higher). Beyond these conclusions, it is hard to judge the effects of individual procedures, other than to note that California, the state that omitted far more TDM procedures than others, had by far the lowest response rate. Our general conclusion is that adherence to the entire set of TDM procedures produces the highest response rates, but knowledge of which procedures make the greater difference awaits further testing.

Past research has demonstrated the importance of additional follow-ups for achieving high response (Heberlein and Baumgartner, 1978 and Dillman and others, 1974) and is confirmed by this research. However, similarity in rankings between the adherence index and measures of survey effectiveness go beyond differences attributable to the presence or absence of that follow-up.

Based on these findings, we recommend that research be done which varies details of the TDM experimentally in otherwise identical surveys using the same survey instrument in independent samples from a single population.

References

Dillman, D. A. *Mail and Telephone Surveys: The Total Design Method.* New York: Wiley-Interscience, 1978.

Dillman, D. A., Christenson, J. A., Carpenter, E. H., and Brooks, R. M. "Increasing Mail Questionnaire Response: A Four-State Comparison." *American Sociological Review,* 1974, *39*, 744–756.

Dillman, D. A., and Moore, D. E. "Improving Response to Mail Surveys: Results from Five Surveys." Unpublished manuscript, 1983.

Heberlein, T. A., and Baumgartner, R. "Factors Affecting Response Rates to Mailed Questionnaires: A Quantitative Analysis of the Published Literature." *American Sociological Review,* 1978, *43*, 447–462.

Makela, C. J., Chatelain, L. B., Dillman, D. A., Dillman, J. J., and Tripple, P. A. *Energy Directions for the United States: A Western Perspective.* Corvallis, Ore.: Western Rural Development Center, 1982.

Don A. Dillman is a professor in the Department of Sociology and a research and extension scientist in the Department of Rural Sociology at Washington State University.

Joye J. Dillman is an assistant professor in the Department of Child and Family Studies at Washington State University.

Carole J. Makela is an associate professor and head of the Department of Consumer Sciences and Housing at Colorado State University.

Three regression approaches are compared and the authors
review the literature on return rates.

Recent Research on Mailed
Questionnaire Response Rates

Robert M. Baumgartner
Thomas A. Heberlein

In 1978, we published an article (Heberlein and Baumgartner, 1978) that was a quantitative review of 214 mailed surveys. Since that time, about forty additional studies of mailed surveys, including two replications of our original work, have been conducted. This chapter reviews these new studies to access advances in research on mailed questionnaires over the last five years.

In our original study, we coded seventy-one factors reported in methodological studies of mailed questionnaires and examined their effect on response rates. Through analysis, we reduced the seventy-one factors to ten variables, which predicted 66 percent of the variability in final response rate. Subsequently, Goyder (1982) replicated our analysis and procedures on an intended data set that included more than 330 surveys, and Eichner and Habermehl (1981) attempted to replicate our model on an independent sample of 152 mailed surveys from Austria and West Germany. We will use the ten variables in Table 1 to organize the review. Research that does not fall into these categories will be discussed separately.

Sponsorship

In our original analysis (Heberlein and Baumgartner, 1978), studies sponsored by a market research organization had a 10 percent lower response

D. C. Lockhart (Ed.). *Making Effective Use of Mailed Questionnaires.*
New Directions for Program Evaluation, no. 21. San Francisco: Jossey-Bass, March 1984.

Table 1. Comparison of Three Regression Models Predicting
Final Return Rate on Mailed Questionnaires
Unstandarized Coefficients

Independent Variables	Heberlein and Baumgartner (1978)	Goyder (1982)	Eichner and Habermehl (1981)
Constant	36.3	24.7	18.9
Market Research Background	− 10.1	− 1.6	− 10.0
Government Organization	10.2	13.7	− 45.8
General Population	− 7.5	− 1.1	− 6.5
Employee Populations	11.8	2.0	.1
School or Army Population	9.9	6.3	11.3
Salience of Topic	7.3	12.2	7.9
Number of Pages	− .4	− .4	7.2
Total Number of Contacts	7.4	7.8	5.6
Special Third Contact	8.6	4.3	1.9
Incentive-First Contact	6.1	7.5	.3
$r \pm$	.66	.64	.49

rate than others, while government sponsored, including university-sponsored studies, obtained a 10 percent higher response rate. With his extended sample, Goyder (1982) replicated the effect of government sponsorship, but the negative effect of market research sponsorship essentially disappeared. The findings of Eichner and Habermehl (1981) suggest possible cross-cultural differences, since both government and market research sponsorship reduced response rates. Heberlein and Baumgartner (1981b) and Goyder (1982) discuss the limitations of the European research.

Research by Jones and his associates (Jones, 1979; Jones and Linda, 1978; Jones and Lang, 1980, 1982) supports our original conclusion about the relative effects of government and university sponsorship and market research sponsorship. Although their base response rates were very low (25 to 35 percent), they found that university sponsorship increased response rate by 6 to 10 percent over sponsorship by a private market research firm.

In contrast, Hawkins (1979) found that surveys sponsored by a university or a private research firm did equally well, and both types of sponsorship yielded significantly higher response rates than department store sponsorship of the same survey. This finding is consistent with Goyder's (1982). We can conclude that, at least in the United States and Canada, government and university sponsorship should enhance response. Market research firm identification may decrease response rate; at best, it does not affect it.

Jones (1979) adds additional information that helps to document the effect of sponsorship and that suggests how it influences response. He found an important interaction between respondent's location and type of sponsorship. In the areas immediately adjacent to the sponsoring university, response rates were about 11 percent higher than rates for government agency sponsorship, but in another area surrounding a different university, government agency sponsorship produced an even higher response rate. He speculates that regional loyalties and competing universities may temper the effect of university sponsorship in some areas. The implication is that those who use mailed questionnaires should use the form of sponsorship that has the highest prestige for the target population. In statewide surveys, prestige can vary by locations.

Respondents

In 1978, we reported lower returns when general populations were surveyed and higher returns when employee, school, or army populations were surveyed. Our findings for the general population were replicated in Europe by Eichner and Habermehl (1981), but they were not replicated by Goyder (1982), and our finding on employee populations was not replicated by Goyder or by Eichner and Habermehl. All these studies show that higher response rates should be expected if respondents are in school or army populations. We found no new case studies comparing response rates from mailed surveys to two different populations.

Salience

In 1978, we found that salience had a powerful effect on response. Surveys judged to be highly salient to respondents obtained a 77 percent response rate, surveys judged to be possibly salient obtained a 66 percent response rate, and surveys judged not to be salient obtained a 42 percent response rate. In the ten-variable model, each increase in the three-point salience scale increased final responses by 7.3 percent.

The same effect holds both in Goyder's (1982) extension and in the European replications (Eichner and Habermehl, 1981). It can safely be said that salient surveys get higher responses. What now needs to be done is to test procedures that increase the perceived salience of surveys. Between 1978 and 1983, there were no experimental or quasi-experimental tests of the salience construct.

Follow-Up Contacts

Follow-up contacts have been recognized for more than sixty years as an effective way of increasing response rates (Lindsey, 1921). In 1978, we found that the number of contacts was the best single predictor of final response rate ($r = .634$, $p_x.001$), since it accounted for nearly 42 percent of the variance in final response rate. In the ten-variable model, each contact increased response by 7.4 percent. This strong effect was replicated both by Goyder (1982) and by Eichner and Habermehl (1981). Yu and Cooper (1983) also document this effect.

Recent studies have examined the effect of appeals in combination with contacts and the effectiveness of including a second copy of the questionnaire with the contact. Goulet (1977) looked at the effect of various appeals in a follow-up letter to a sample of exhibit managers for a national trade show. An appeal asking the respondent to explain why no response had been given to the first mailing and offering another chance to respond produced the greatest number of replies. However, this appeal resulted in no more usable responses than appeals to complete the questionnaire or appeals to complete specific parts of the questionnaire. Comer and Kelly (1980) tested the relative effectiveness of telephone and mail follow-ups with a sample of real estate professionals. These investigators found that telephone follow-ups produced a higher response rate (46 percent versus 33 percent, p_x.10). Jolson (1977) reports that prenotification by telephone, analogous to an advance letter, produced a higher than anticipated response rate in a survey of households, although no control group was used for comparison.

Swan and others (1980) and Heberlein and Baumgartner (1981a) examined a practical issue in the use of follow-up contacts: Is it necessary to include a copy of the questionnaire in follow-up mailings? Swan and others (1980) found in a survey of real estate professionals that including a copy of the questionnaire in the first follow-up mailing produced no increase in response (7.5 percent versus 7.7 percent of possible returns), but it was nearly twice as effective on a second follow-up mailing (8 percent versus 4.3 percent).

Heberlein and Baumgartner (1981b) report thirteen independent experiments that contrasted the effects of using a letter and a questionnaire in a follow-up mailing with the effects of using a letter only. Overall, the treatments that coupled a letter with a questionnaire produced a 30.4 percent response rate, while the treatments that used only a letter yielded a 27.5 percent response rate. These studies suggest that including a questionnaire in a follow-up mailing can be expected to increase response rates slightly, but in some instances that increase may not be justified by the cost.

As Table 1 shows, Heberlein and Baumgartner (1978) and Goyder (1982) found that use of a special class of mail in follow-up contacts increases response rates. Eichner and Habermehl (1981) did not find this to be true in their European sample. No research has examined this question.

Incentives

Of the ten variables, the use of incentives to increase response rates has received the most attention. Our finding in 1978 that each 25 cent incentive increased the response rate by 6 percent was replicated by Goyder (1982). Eichner and Habermehl (1981) found no effects from incentives in the European studies.

McDaniel and Rao (1980) found that a prepaid incentive of 25 cents described as a token of appreciation was more effective than no incentive, and Hansen (1980) found that a prepaid monetary incentive of 25 cents was more effective than an enclosed ballpoint pen of comparable value and that both were more effective than no incentive. Goodstadt and others (1977) found that use of a prepaid incentive of 25 cents in a survey of Canadian magazine subscribers increased the final response rate more than an enclosed book, a promised book, or no incentive.

Two studies have examined the effectiveness of offering a contribution to a charity of the respondent's choice as an incentive for responding. Robertson and Bellenger (1978) compared the effects of a promised $1 monetary incentive and of a promised $1 contribution to charity. The promised contribution to charity yielded a higher response to a single mailing (41.3 percent) than the promised monetary incentive (26 percent) and than no incentive (23.3 percent). The last two response rates were not statistically different.

Furse and Stewart (1982) compared a promised $1 charitable contribution with no contribution and prepaid monetary incentives of 50 cents and $1 with no incentive in a two-by-three experimental design. They found no main effect for the promised charitable contribution; the response rate for no contribution was 66 percent, while the response rate for the $1 contribution was 68.3 percent. However, a strong linear effect was found for the prepaid monetary incentive.

Two studies conducted in the Netherlands by Nederhof (1983) found that a nonmonetary incentive was more effective for a sample drawn from a university's volunteer subject pool than it was for a general sample of the university community.

One issue in the use of incentives that we found in 1978 to have received very little attention was effectiveness of incentives included not in the first mailing but in a follow-up contact. Furse and others (1977) compared the effectiveness of a prepaid monetary incentive of 50 cents on the first mailing with its effectiveness on a follow-up mailing and on both contacts. The researchers found no difference between the three treatment groups; final response rates were 52 percent, 54 percent, and 51 percent, respectively. All three treatment groups had a higher response rate than the control group, whose response rate was 39 percent.

Tedin and Hofstetter (1982) tested the effectiveness of a prepaid incentive of 25 cents on the first mailing with its effectiveness on two follow-up contacts. They found that, with a single follow-up contact, an enclosing incentive with the first mailing produced a higher return than enclosing the same incentive with the follow-up contact. With a second follow-up mailing, these differences largely disappeared. These data suggest that it may be more cost-effective to use a prepaid incentive on follow-up contacts than on the initial mailing.

A second question that remains unanswered is the effect of larger incentives, either prepaid or promised, on response rates. There is very little evidence on the effect of incentives greater than $1. Armstrong (1975) noted that a large-scale survey examining the effect of incentives ranging as high as $10 or $20 on a number of different populations would be helpful. Such a study still needs to be done. Godwin (1979) reports a survey of elites in sixty countries in which no incentive and incentives of $25 and $50 were used. He found a 10 percent increment in response for the $25 incentive and a 1 percent increment for the $50 incentive. The unusual sample and the potential cultural differences among respondents make it difficult to generalize from his findings.

Length

The effect of the length of a questionnaire on response rate has been the subject of much research, but no widely accepted explanation of its effect has emerged. Longer questionnaires have higher costs to respondents, but longer questionnaires may also signal to respondents that the study is important (Heberlein and Baumgartner, 1978).

Heberlein and Baumgartner (1978) found that the length of a questionnaire measured by the number of pages, the number of items, or the estimated time of completion had no zero-order relationship with the final response rate. After the number of contacts and the salience of the topic to respondents were controlled, length showed a modest negative effect on response rate. Yu and Cooper (1983) and Goyder (1982) report similar findings. Eichner and Habermehl (1981) found a positive effect for length in their review of European studies.

Two experiments have examined the effect of length on response rate. In a survey of members of the American Marketing Association, Childers and Ferrell (1979) tested the effects of one- and two-page questionnaires and of $8\frac{1}{2}" \times 11"$ and $8\frac{1}{2}" \times 14"$ pages. The size of the pages had a significant negative effect on response rate, but the effect of the number of pages was not significant.

Hornik (1981) examined the effect of a time cue in the cover letter on response rate. Telling respondents that it would take twenty minutes to complete the questionnaire produced a 41.5 percent response rate with a single mailing while a forty-minute time cue produced a 25.5 percent response rate. A control group that did not receive a time cue had a 31.5 percent response rate on the same six-page, thirty-five-item instrument.

The effect of a wide range of questionnaire lengths on response rate needs to be examined. The issue of length also needs to be investigated from the respondent's point of view. The evidence to date seems to indicate that the modest negative effect of length on final response rate can be overcome if other procedures, such as follow-up contacts or incentives, are also used.

Other Variables

Anonymity. The literature on the use of anonymous procedures, which goes back five decades, shows conflicting results (Skinner and Childers, 1980), but it does not appear that anonymous procedures are necessary in order to obtain high response rates. In 1978, we did not find that anonymous procedures enhanced response rates, and in this finding we are seconded by Yu and Cooper (1983). Skinner and Childers (1980) found that more than 90 percent of the respondents to an anonymous questionnaire put their return address on the envelope in which they returned it. There were no differences in the data provided by the anonymous and nonanonymous groups. However, Jones (1979) showed that, even when there was no overall effect of anonymity, there were differences by county of residence. In the highest-income areas, anonymity increased response by 8.3 percent, while in areas of high population change, anonymity decreased responses by 8.1 percent.

Anonymity may be important in some instances, such as in surveys of employees or surveys of particular groups of people who would not want their membership in the group to be known. However, Futrell and Swan (1977) found that employees of a national organization were just as likely to return a questionnaire that bore an identification number as they were to return one that guaranteed anonymity.

Personalization. Some researchers, such as Dillman (1978), suggest that personalization of cover letters and mailing envelopes affects response rates positively. In 1978, we did not find that personalization had any effect on final or initial response rates. Studies by LaBrecque (1978) and by Roberts and others (1978) failed to show that positive effects could be attributed to personalization in surveys of potential users of an East Cove marina and of members of a professional organization. However, Yu and Cooper (1983) found a positive association between personalization and response rate, although it is unclear how many of the studies that they analyzed used mailed questionnaires and how many used telephone or personal interviews. Their review of experimental studies showed that the treatment group had a 6.6 percent higher response rate than the control groups across thirty-five studies. Given this conflicting evidence, it seems likely that anonymous procedures and personalization interact with other factors, such as the type of population surveyed, the topic of the survey, or the sponsor. More attention needs to be given to multifactor studies, so that we can specify when these procedures increase response rates and when they do not.

Deadline. Two studies have examined the effectiveness of using a deadline to enhance response rates. Vocino (1977) found no effect for a deadline of less than two weeks on a single mailing. However, Roberts and others (1978) found that a three-week deadline increased responses to an initial mailing and to a first follow-up mailing but that the difference was not significant after the second follow-up. Both studies surveyed members of a professional association.

Types of Appeals. Jones and Linda (1978) and Childers and others (1980) studied the effectiveness of various types of appeals in a cover letter. Jones and Linda found that appeals emphasizing benefits to respondents and benefits to science both produced higher response rates than appeals to help the survey sponsor—in this case, resort parks in Kentucky.

Childers and others (1980) surveyed two samples: a group of academics who belonged to a professional association and a group of business persons who subscribed to a newsletter. For the sample of academics, they found that an appeal emphasizing the benefits to respondents and an appeal to help the sponsor produced higher responses than an appeal to the social benefits of the research. However, the response rate was highest for the control group, which received no appeal. In the survey of business persons, no differences were found among the four treatment groups.

Postage. The effect on response rates of the class of postage at which questionnaires are mailed continues to attract the attention of researchers. Our search of the recent literature uncovered seven new studies plus a quantitative review of the literature by Armstrong and Lusk (1983).

The class of postage that produces the best response rate has not been clearly established. Armstrong and Lusk (1983) note that, of earlier reviews of return postage studies, two recommended the use of first-class stamps, one recommended the use of business reply postage, and one concluded that the results were inconsistent. In the seven new studies that we reviewed, the response rates are low, and the differences between treatment groups tend to be small.

Gaffey (1978) compared use of first-class stamps on the return envelope with business reply postage for a single mailing and found a statistically significant 6 percent increase in response rate when first-class stamps were used. Jones and Linda (1978) and Wolfe and Treiman (1979) tested the relative effects of commemorative stamps, regular first-class postage, business reply postage, and metered postage. Both studies found that regular first-class stamps and commemorative stamps yielded slightly higher response rates. In contrast, LaBrecque (1978), Brook (1978), and McCrohan and Lowe (1981) found that the type of postage used on the return envelope produced no differences. Most studies have concluded that business reply postage is cost-effective on a cost-per-respondent basis. However, Armstrong and Lusk's (1983) quantitative review suggests that regular first-class and commemorative stamps can expect the same results and that both produce a greater response rate than business reply or metered postage on the return envelope.

Tests of the effectiveness of different classes of postage on the outer mailing envelope have typically contrasted first-class with third-class or metered first-class and metered third-class postage. However, it seems unwise differences between commemorative stamps, regular first-class stamps, and metered postage. McCrohan and Lowe (1981) also found no differences between metered first-class and metered third-class postage. However, it seems unwise to use third-class mail unless one is very confident that all the names and addresses on one's sample list are valid.

Tedin and Hofstetter (1982) found that the use of certified mail for the first mailing produced a substantial increment in the response rate (26 percent versus 14 percent) but that the use of certified mail on a single follow-up contact produced an even higher cumulative response (52 percent versus 44 percent). If multiple contacts are planned, it certainly seems advisable to use certified mail only on a follow-up contact.

Summary

Studies conducted since 1978 show that government or university sponsorship increases response rate and that market research sponsorship may not decrease response. European and U.S. results on sponsorship appear to differ. Sponsorship may have different effects on different groups in the same survey. A belief among respondents in the prestige and credibility of the sponsor appears to enhance response rates. It also appears that high response rates are possible in the general population, although research continues to show that response rates to mailed surveys are higher for school and army populations.

Our study of 1978 was the first to show the dramatic effect of salience to respondents on overall response. This finding was replicated on an independent sample of European surveys and on an extended sample of North American mailed surveys. No subsequent work has examined the effects of salience. At the very least, experiments aimed at increasing the perceived salience to respondents should be conducted in order to examine the effects on response rate.

The well-known positive effects of follow-up contacts were also replicated in Europe. However, while it seldoms hurts response rate to include a questionnaire in a second mailing, it may not always be cost-effective to do so.

Incentives have been the object of a good deal of research. It is certainly worth paying respondents 25 cents or $1 in advance. However, a payment works even if it is included only in the second mailing. More research needs to be done on the effects of larger amounts, such as $3 and $5.

The very modest negative effect of length on response rates continues to be documented. In one study, the perception of length was shown to affect response rate.

The effects of anonymity and personalization are still not clear. It appears that these factors interact with characteristics both of respondents and of surveys to increase or decrease responses. Time deadlines can increase response rates. Finally, while the data are mixed, it appears that first-class postage produced better results than business or metered postage.

Thus, while further quantitative reviews, cross-cultural comparisons, useful work on incentives, and some studies that examined interactions have produced some advances in our knowledge of response rates to mailed questionnaires, many of the criticisms that we made in 1978 still hold. For example, there has still been no large-scale multivariate experiment. Much of the research continues to be restricted to a single experimental treatment, and there has been little effort to develop a theory of mailed questionnaire response rates.

References

Armstrong, J. S. "Monetary Incentives in Mail Surveys." *Public Opinion Quarterly,* 1975, *39,* 111–116.

Armstrong, J. S., and Lusk, E. J. "The Effect of Return Postage on Mail Survey Response: A Quantitative Review." Unpublished manuscript, Department of Marketing, University of Pennsylvania, 1983.

Brook, L. L. "The Effect of Different Postage Combinations on Response Levels and Speed of Reply." *Journal of the Market Research Society,* 1978, *20* (4), 239–244.

Childers, T. L., and Ferrell, O. C. "Response Rates and Perceived Questionnaire Length in Mail Surveys." *Journal of Marketing Research,* 1979, *16,* 429–431.

Childers, T. L., Pride, W. M., and Ferrell, O. C. "A Reassessment of the Effects of Appeals on Response to Mail Surveys." *Journal of Marketing Research,* 1980, *17,* 365–370.

Comer, J. M., and Kelly, J. S. "Follow-up Techniques: The Effect of Methods and Source Appeal." Working paper, University of Cincinnati, 1980.

Dillman, D. A. *Mail and Telephone Surveys: The Total Design Method.* New York: Wiley-Interscience, 1978.

Eichner, K., and Habermehl, W. "Predicting Response Rates to Mailed Questionnaires (Comment on Heberlein and Baumgartner, *ASR,* August 1978)." *American Sociological Review,* 1981, *46,* 361–363.

Furse, D. H., and Stewart, D. W. "Monetary Incentives Versus Promised Contributions to Charity: New Evidence on Mailed Survey Response." *Journal of Marketing Research,* 1982, *19,* 375–380.

Furse, D. H., Stewart, D. W., and Rados, D. L. "Effects of Foot in the Door, Cash Incentives, and Follow-ups on Survey Response." *Journal of Marketing Research,* 1977, *14,* 611–616.

Gaffey, H. J., Jr. "Questionnaire Returns: Stamps Versus Business Reply Envelopes Revisited." *Journal of Marketing Research,* 1978, *15,* 290–293.

Godwin, R. K. "The Consequences of Large Monetary Incentives in Mail Surveys of Elites." *Public Opinion Quarterly,* 1979, *43,* 378–387.

Goodstadt, M. S., Chung, L., Cronity, R., and Cook, G. "Mail Survey Response Rates: Their Manipulation and Impact." *Journal of Marketing Research,* 1977, *14,* 391–395.

Goulet, W. M. "Efficacy of a Third Request Letter in Mail Surveys of Professionals." *Journal of Marketing Research,* 1977, *14,* 112–114.

Goyder, J. C. "Further Evidence on Factors Affecting Response Rates to Mailed Questionnaires." *American Sociological Review,* 1982, *47,* 550–553.

Hansen, R. A. "A Self-Perception Interpretation of the Effect of Monetary and Nonmonetary Incentives on Mail Survey Respondent Behavior." *Journal of Marketing Research,* 1980, *17,* 77–83.

Hawkins, D. I. "The Impact of Sponsor Identification and Direct Disclosure of Respondent Rights on the Quantity and Quality of Mail Survey Data." *Journal of Business,* 1979, *52* (4), 577–590.

Heberlein, T. A., and Baumgartner, R. M. "Factors Affecting Response Rates to Mailed Questionnaires: A Quantitative Analysis of the Published Literature." *American Sociological Review,* 1978, *43* (4), 447–462.

Heberlein, T. A., and Baumgartner, R. M. "Is a Questionnaire Necessary in a Second Mailing?" *Public Opinion Quarterly*, 1981a, *45*, 102–108.

Heberlein, T. A., and Baumgartner, R. M. "The Effectiveness of the Heberlein-Baumgartner Models for Predicting Response Rates to Mailed Questionnaires: European and U.S. Examples." *American Sociological Review*, 1981b, *46*, 361–363.

Hornik, J. "Time Cue and Time Perception Effect on Response to Mail Surveys." *Journal of Marketing Research*, 1981, *18*, 243–248.

Houston, M. J., and Nevin, J. R. "The Effects of Source and Appeal on Mailed Survey Response Patterns." *Journal of Marketing Research*, 1977, *14*, 374–378.

Jolson, M. A. "How to Double or Triple Mail Survey Response Rates." *Journal of Marketing*, 1977, *41*, 78–81.

Jones, W. H. "Generalizing Mail Survey Inducement Methods: Population Interactions with Anonymity and Sponsorship." *Public Opinion Quarterly*, 1979, *43*, 102–111.

Jones, W. H., and Lang, J. R. "Sample Composition Bias and Response Bias in a Mail Survey: A Comparison of Inducement Methods." *Journal of Marketing Research*, 1980, *17*, 69–76.

Jones, W. H., and Lang, J. R. "Reliability and Validity Effects Under Mail Survey Conditions." *Journal of Business Research*, 1982, *10*, 339–353.

Jones, W. H., and Linda, G. "Multiple Criteria Effects in a Mail Survey Experiment." *Journal of Marketing Research*, 1978, *15*, 280–284.

LaBrecque, D. P. "A Response Rate Experiment Using Mail Questionnaires." *Journal of Marketing*, 1978, *42*, 82–83.

Lindsey, E. E. "Questionnaires and Follow-up Letters." *Pedagogical Seminary Journal*, 1921, *28*, 303–307.

McCrohan, K. F., and Lowe, L. S. "A Cost-Benefit Approach to Postage Used in Mail Questionnaires." *Journal of Marketing*, 1981, *45*, 130–133.

McDaniel, S. W., and Rao, C. P. "The Effect of Monetary Inducement on Mailed Questionnaire Response Quality." *Journal of Marketing Research*, 1980, *17*, 265–268.

Nederhof, A. J. "The Effects of Material Incentives in Mailed Surveys: Two Studies." *Public Opinion Quarterly*, 1983, *47*, 103–111.

Roberts, R. E., McCrory, O. F., and Forthofer, R. N. "Further Evidence on Using a Deadline to Stimulate Responses to a Mail Survey." *Public Opinion Quarterly*, 1978, *42*, 407–410.

Robertson, D. H., and Bellenger, D. N. "A New Method of Increasing Mail Survey Responses: Contributions to Charity." *Journal of Marketing Research*, 1978, *15*, 632–633.

Skinner, S. J., and Childers, T. L. "Respondent Identification in Mail Surveys." *Journal of Advertising Research*, 1980, *20* (6), 57–61.

Swan, J. E., Epley, D. E., and Burns, W. L. "Can Follow-up Response Rates to a Mail Survey Be Increased by Including Another Copy of the Questionnaire?" *Psychological Reports*, 1980, *47*, 103–106.

Tedin, K. L., and Hofstetter, C. R. "The Effect of Cost and Importance Factors on the Return Rate for Single and Multiple Mailings." *Public Opinion Quarterly*, 1982, *46*, 122–128.

Vocino, T. "Three Variables in Stimulating Response to Mailed Questionaires." *Journal of Marketing*, 1977, *41*, 76–77.

Wolfe, A. C., and Treiman, B. R. "Postage Types and Response Rates in Mail Surveys." *Journal of Advertising Research*, 1979, *19* (1), 43–48.

Yu, J., and Cooper, H. "A Quantitative Review of Research Design Effects on Response Rates to Questionnaires." *Journal of Marketing Research*, 1983, *20*, 36–44.

Robert M. Baumgartner is a research analyst with Heberlein-Baumgartner Research Services, Madison, Wisconsin.

Thomas A. Heberlein is professor in the Department of Rural Sociology, University of Wisconsin, Madison.

This chapter applies theories from several disciplines
to the mailed questionnaire methodology.

Applying Attitude Theories to the Return of Mailed Questionnaires

Jack McKillip

About seven years ago, I confronted the need to use a mailed survey as part of an evaluation. I had agreed to evaluate a three-year responsible alcohol use intervention program on a college campus, and I wanted to collect yearly information on students' alcohol use. A mailed survey of a large random sample of students seemed to be the best way of gathering that information. I needed to know when to mail what and to whom in order to maximize the return of the survey questionnaires, but I was disappointed when I reviewed the many procedures that have been used to increase the return of mailed questionnaires. There were few strong effects, there were many contradictory findings, and there was no theory. The first two facts were probably related to the third: Trial and error promotes evolution and progress, but the process itself is inefficient. A number of the writers whom I consulted decried the absence of theoretical guidance (Heberlein and Baumgartner, 1978; Linsky, 1975).

Reviews by Heberlein and Baumgartner (1978) and by Yu and Cooper (1983) point to three factors that consistently affect the return of mailed questionnaires. Respondents' interest in the questionnaire topic, the number of contacts with respondents, and the use of a small monetary incentive routinely

D. C. Lockhart (Ed.). *Making Effective Use of Mailed Questionnaires.*
New Directions for Program Evaluation, no. 21. San Francisco: Jossey-Bass, March 1984.

produce important increases in return rates. Little seems to be known about why these factors increase the target behavior while other variables do not. Furse and Stewart (1982) used cognitive dissonance theory to explain the effects of monetary incentives, and some version of social exchange theory (Berkowitz and Walster, 1976) may also be useful here. However, past attempts to explain these effects have focused on a single or very few survey procedures, and they have not offered much general guidance.

Why Attitude Theories?

Attitude — an enduring predisposition to behave in a certain manner — is the primary theoretical construct that social psychologists use to explain the relationship between events that an individual confronts, such as receipt of a mailed questionnaire, and the individual's behavior, such as returning or not returning the questionnaire. However, after Wicker's (1969) critical review of research on the relationship between atitude and behavior, many questioned the usefulness of attitude in understanding and predicting behavior. During the last decade, both theoretical and methodological advances have answered most of the questions, and they have demonstrated that attitude-like constructs can predict behavior accurately, even over a period of years (Ajzen and Fishbein, 1977). One of the most interesting theoretical refinements of the attitude construct is the notion of behavioral intention. For Fishbein and Ajzen (1976), behavioral intention mediates between attitude and behavior; for Triandis (1977, 1980), it replaces the notion of attitude in scientific discussion. I will use both conceptions in the discussion of the return of mailed questionnaires that follows.

Another aspect of attitude that has come in for attention is the individual's involvement in the issue (Sherif, 1980). The concept of involvement is quite similar to the factor that Heberlein and Baumgartner (1978) found to be the single best predictor of the return of a mailed questionnaire, respondents' interest in the topic of the questionnaire. I will apply two theories that are relevant to this notion: Rothchild's discussions of advertising strategy (1979a, 1979b) and Katz's (1960) functional theory. My discussion of both behavioral intention and involvement will be speculative, so for some it may be less than satisfying. However, at this stage in the development of relevant theory, the attitude construct can be an important heuristic for research on the return of mailed questionnaires.

Behavioral Intentions

For the theory of reasoned action (Fishbein and Ajzen, 1976; Ajzen and Fishbein, 1980), the behavior of returning a mailed questionnaire is best predicted from an individual's behavioral intention — the subjective likelihood that the individual will engage in a given behavior. Predictive accuracy increases if the behavioral intention and the behavior are measured at the same level of specificity. For example, the behavior of returning a mailed questionnaire (action) about health behaviors (target) to a local hospital (context) within the next two weeks (time) is best predicted from an individual's *intention* to return a mailed questionnaire about health behaviors to a local hospital within the next two weeks. Behavioral intention is an internal construct that mediates between an individual's attitude and the individual's behavior.

General attitudes, such as attitudes toward health behaviors or the survey sponsor, and specific behavioral intentions, such as the intention to return a mailed questionnaire about health behaviors to the local hospital within the next two weeks, are not related. Behavioral intention (BI) is determined both by an individual's attitude toward the behavior (A_B) (that is, where action, target, context, and time are consistent between attitude and intention) and by the individual's perceptions of whether important others expect the individual to engage in the behavior (SN). BI can be predicted from equation 1:

$$(1) \qquad\qquad BI = w_1{}^*A_B + w_2{}^*SN$$

where w_1 and w_2 are empirically determined weights reflecting the importance of the determinants of *BI*. The intention to return a mailed questionnaire is hypothesized to be due to the individual's attitude toward returning that questionnaire and to the expectations that the individual perceives others to hold for his or her return of the questionnaire. Variables that affect return rate must operate through A_B, SN, or both, and variables that affect either construct will affect return rates.

A_B is determined by the individual's perceptions of the salient consequences of the behavior. Respondents will have a positive attitude toward return of a questionnaire if they perceive that return will lead to positive consequences, and they will have a negative attitude if they perceive that the consequences of return are negative. Return rate will be affected by variables that either present potential respondents with or that remind them of positive consequences of return of the questionnaire, such as the social utility cover letters described by Houston and Nevin (1977) or that counter the perception of negative consequences, such as inclusion of return postage. SN is determined by the expectations concerning return of the questionnaire that the respondent perceives important others to hold. Return rates will be affected by factors that bring to mind groups or individuals who have an opinion about the return of questionnaires by potential respondents. Identifying the sponsorship of a questionnaire is a procedure that can affect SN.

Ajzen and Fishbein (1980) suggest that the positive and negative consequences of behavior and the expectations of important individuals and groups can be determined by interviews of those who might engage in the behavior. Thus, a sample of potential survey respondents could be asked what they perceive to be the advantages and disadvantages of returning—and of not returning—a mailed questionnaire. The researcher could then use this information to make the perceived advantages salient and to overcome the perceived disadvantages. Lockhart (personal communication) tried this procedure in designing a questionnaire concerning political opinions. Less than 20 percent of those whom he interviewed were able to generate any consequences for return of a mailed questionnaire or to identify individuals or groups who would have expectations about how respondents should behave. This finding suggests that respondents begin with a neutral behavioral intention for the return of a questionnaire. Survey procedures that will lead to a positive BI should be selected.

Certain procedures can be expected to create the impression of positive consequences for return: promising results or some other premium that is contingent on return of the questionnaire, emphasizing the utility of findings obtained from the questionnaire either to society or to individual respondents, and making salient the opportunity afforded to respondents to express their personal opinions. Other procedures can be expected to counter the impression of negative consequences: using a short or at least a seemingly short questionnaire, including a return envelope and return postage, and developing a layout and question format that minimize the impression that the questionnaire will be tedious to complete. It is more difficult to predict the effect of survey procedures on SN, since respondents' reactions depend not only on the salience of others' expectations but also on motivation to comply with these expectations. For example, identifying the sponsor of the questionnaire will be helpful to the extent that potential respondents feel motivated to comply with the sponsor's expectations. Many mailed survey procedures seem to affect not the direction of SN but its importance (that is, w_2 in equation 1). Guarantees of the confidentiality of results, anonymous return, and third-class postage probably make SN less important, whereas use of first-class postage and personalization of the envelope and the cover letter should increase the importance of this component. Unfortunately, Fishbein (1980) offers little guidance on individual variables that affect the relative importance of the A_B and the SN components.

In a manner quite out of step with recent theoretical statements in the social sciences, Triandis (1977, 1980) has proposed a general theory of interpersonal behavior that includes history, ecology, culture, and genetics in addition to personality and behavior. The aspects of that theory which are of greatest interest are the parts that indicate "the conditions under which either strong or weak relationships between verbal attitudes and behavior are likely to be observed" (Triandis, 1980, p. 197). Triandis rejects the construct of attitude for scientific discourse and replaces it with behavioral intention—the instructions that people give to themselves to behave in certain ways. For behaviors with which people have little experience (such as the return of mailed questionnaires), behavioral intention is the primary personal determinant of behavior. Behavioral intention *(BI)* is determined by three factors: social factors *(S)*, which reflect the expectations of important others, reference groups, and so forth; affect *(A)*, the direct emotional response to the thought of the behavior; and the consequences of the behavior *(C)*, the subjective utility of the behavior. The relationship of these factors to *BI* are shown in equation 2:

(2) $$BI = S + A + C$$

The primary difference between equation 2 and equation 1 is that Triandis divides Fishbein and Ajzen's (1976) attitude toward behavior *(A_B)* into *A* and *C* factors. These factors represent a division between immediate, here-and-now, time-limited satisfactions *(A)* and future, longer-lasting satisfactions *(C)*. This distinction between immediate and future satisfactions proves to be quite useful in predicting the effects of survey procedures on return rates.

Noting that most mailed questionnaires involve impersonal mailing and anonymous return, Triandis (1980) suggests that the *S* component will have little effect on return rates. Also, since the future consequences of return of the questionnaire are unclear to potential respondents, the *C* component will be of little importance. These considerations lead to the prediction that mailed questionnaire return will be due primarily to *A* — the immediate emotional response that respondents have to the questionnaire. In this case, positive affect is encouraged by opportunities to express personal opinions, by opportunities to express the truth, or by both. Negative affect, which might be expected to be more powerful, could be caused by the time that it takes to complete the questionnaire, by the tedium of completing the questionnaire, and by the expense of returning the questionnaire. In the hypothetical survey situation that I have sketched here, those who are most likely to return the questionnaire are those who are most committed to a position on the topic of the survey, since they are the only ones for whom there is much positive affect. This prediction is consistent with Heberlein and Baumgartner's (1978) between-survey finding that respondents' interest in a questionnaire greatly facilitates return.

Another hypothesis consistent with this simple affect model is that incentives operate by creating positive affect, which in turn facilitates the intention to complete and return the questionnaire. In keeping with Triandis's definition of A, the effects of incentives can be expected to be short-lived.

The importance of *A* for determining the intention to return a questionnaire can be lessened by procedures that make the *S* or *C* factors more important. Techniques that identify the recipient personally or in terms of some group will make the expectations and norms of the culture or of the particular reference group more salient. The interpersonal relationships could be emphasized by prominent identification of sponsorship and by explicit mention in a cover letter. If the recipient has internalized a norm of social reciprocity, inclusion of an incentive with the questionnaire may be particularly useful in encouraging return.

Making the C factor more important may be difficult in the context of a mailed questionnaire, since the behavior of return is actually quite free. The promise of some incentive or of a summary of results might help, but research has not indicated that these procedures have much effect. Making explicit the prospect of numerous follow-ups to recipients who do not return the questionnaire might impose a future consequence on nonreturn and thereby encourage return. Certainly numerous follow-ups have been effective in raising return rates.

In addition to identifying the three predicting factors of equation 2, Triandis (1980) has hypothesized differences between individuals in sensitivity to each of the factors that affect BI. While justification for the hypothesized personality differences is too complex to be summarized here, the differences lead to interesting predictions about the type of respondent who is more likely than others to respond favorably to specific survey procedures. Besides spurring hypotheses about effects on return rates that will be discussed later in this chapter, personality characteristics that Triandis identifies generate concerns about use of mailed questionnaires to collect evaluation measures that might be expected to have strong personality correlates, such as the measures used to evaluate mental health interventions.

According to Triandis (1980), those most likely to respond to S factors are submissive, authoritarian, obedient, and responsible. They are most likely to respond when norms of behavior are clear. These characteristics suggest that members of this group are those least likely to respond to anonymous questionnaires and impersonal mailings and that incentives would attract the biggest response from this group by making a reciprocity norm salient. Those most likely to respond to A factors want an exciting life, they value mature love, and they are imaginative, cognitively simple, and independent. The members of this group should be those most likely to respond to questionnaires that tap their own interests and to aspects of questionnaire layout. Finally, those most likely to respond to C factors take a long time perspective, and they are intelligent and well educated. The members of this group should be those most likely to return a questionnaire when the consequences of return are clear, and they are also those most likely to be affected by the content of a cover letter, since they have the greatest likelihood of reading it and understanding its message.

Involvement

Rothchild (1979a, 1979b) articulates theoretical propositions for the use of advertising procedures that are based on attitude theory and that can heuristically be applied to mailed surveys. Although the analogy to market research is not critical to this discussion, it is interesting: Mailed survey procedures are used to market a product (a questionnaire on a particular topic) that the researcher wants potential respondents to buy (complete and return). According to Rothchild, the critical piece of information in designing an advertising campaign is consumers' level of involvement in the product. Very different strategies should be used when involvement is low and when involvement is high.

Involvement is high when respondents are very interested in the questionnaire topic and when there is a clear difference to the respondent between returning the questionnaire and not returning it. This case is appropriate for classical attitude change strategies (Hovland and others, 1953), which emphasize message content to produce attitude change and then behavior change. Rothchild advocates the use of print media and long messages, low message repetition, and a highly credible source. Applying these recommendations to survey research, we see that the content of the cover letter is important; it should detail the reasons for the study, and it should describe how study data will be used. Follow-ups should be few in number and well separated in time. Finally, sponsorship and endorsements are very important. For the high-involvement purchase, the price of the product is not of prime importance. Thus, the length of the questionnaire and the amount of time that it takes to complete can be discounted.

Involvement is low when respondents have little or no interest in the topic of the questionnaire and when they perceive little difference between returning the questionnaire and not returning it. In this case, consumers are passive, and it will be necessary to get their attention. For Rothchild, a low-involvement strategy should use an approach to attitude change similar to that suggested by Bem (1972), in which awareness leads to behavior that in turn affects attitude. Attitude depends on behavior, not the reverse.

For an effective low-involvement strategy, Rothchild (1979a, 1979b) suggests short messages that convey no more than one or two pieces of information, high message repetition, attention to the visual aspects of packaging (clutter is a problem), and incentives to attract the attention of potential respondents. Thus, the cover letter should be simple. Detailed appeals for cooperation may be harmful. The questionnaire, cover letter, and envelope need to be attractive and well designed. Judicious use of color and white space is called for. Frequent follow-ups and monetary incentives are in order. For the low-involvement purchase, price is the key. Thus, the time needed to complete the questionnaire, its length, and the cost of returning it should be kept to a minimum.

According to Rothchild's theory, the evaluator who uses a mailed questionnaire is in a predicament. If he or she selects high-involvement strategy, there is a good chance that those less interested will not respond. Conversely, if he or she uses the low-involvement strategy, those most likely to contribute may be repelled. Rothchild suggests several alternatives to the low-involvement strategy: portraying the product as controversial, tying into a high-involving issue, and adding attributes to aid discrimination between alternatives. Applying these suggestions to mailed questionnaires, we can imagine adding controversial or interesting questions to the questionnaire, especially to the beginning (Dillman, 1978). Consequences attached to return or nonreturn of the questionnaire might enable potential respondents to perceive differences between these alternatives. Sponsorship or a cover letter could be used to tie completion and return of the questionnaire to some important value held by respondents (McKillip and Lockhart, in press).

Although functional theory (Katz, 1960) has generated only a modest number of empirical studies over the last twenty-five years, it may be particularly useful in suggesting strategies for mailed surveys. The issue is primarily one of motivation. As noted earlier, Heberlein and Baumgartner (1978) found that respondents' interest in a questionnaire was the best predictor of return rate, and Rothchild (1979a, 1979b) suggests that one way of increasing respondents' involvement in a questionnaire is by tying return to some important value that respondents hold. Functional theory suggests motivations or values that might interest respondents in returning a questionnaire.

According to functional theory (Katz, 1960), an individual's attitude and behavior arise from one of four personal motivations or functions. If a behavior, such as return, is perceived as fulfilling one of these four functions, the behavior will be rewarding, and in the context of mailed questionnaires rates should increase. Katz (1960) describes four motivational functions: utility, which reflects an individual's past history of rewards and punishments; value expression, which reflects the reference groups and other symbols that give positive expression to an individual's self-image; knowledge, which arises from an individual's need to make sense of the world; and ego defense, which reflects an individual's attempts to avoid confronting painful stimuli. The conditions under which the functions are invoked are important for their effectiveness in motivating individual behavior. For example, Kelman (1958) found that utility-based messages were most persuasive under conditions of surveillance, that value-expressive messages were most persuasive with attractive sources, and that knowledge messages were most persuasive with expert and trustworthy sources. Any of Katz's four motivations, except perhaps ego defense, may provide a means for generating interest in the return of a mailed questionnaire among potential respondents.

From a utility motivation, respondents will return a questionnaire if they can thereby receive a reward or avoid a punishment. Combining a cover letter that identifies potential rewards to individual respondents with procedures that minimize the anonymity of response—a personalized envelope, a personalized cover letter, nonanonymous return—should maximize this motivation. For the value-expressive function, respondents return a mailed questionnaire because it contributes to their self-image. This motivation should be maximized by sponsorship of the survey by potential respondents' reference groups and by use of their symbols on the questionnaire, the envelope, and the cover letter. Endorsement by a figure popular among the recipients should be helpful. An incentive that ties the respondent to the reference group might be particularly effective. A cover letter that mentions the value of self-expression should also be useful. For the knowledge function, use of a source that has no ulterior motive for gathering the survey data is indicated; thus, a university should be preferred to a marketing research firm. The cover letter should include the reasons for gathering the data and identify any personal insight that the respondent might gain by completing the questionnaire.

McKillip and Lockhart (in press) report two studies that sought to apply functional theory to the design of a cover letter. The value expression appeal produced lower return rates than the knowledge and the utility appeals. The knowledge appeal appeared to facilitate return among some subgroups of those surveyed, while it discouraged return among others.

Discussion

Understanding the factors that determine the return of mailed questionnaires is very important if program evaluators are to use this methodology effectively. While some researchers report consistently high return rates (Dillman, 1978), Yu and Cooper (1983) found that the average return rate for mailed survey studies published between 1965 and 1981 was 47.3 percent. Attrition at this level can cause very serious problems for inferences about program impacts. Beyond the general issue of return rate, the differential effect of survey procedures on returns from various types of evaluation groups has not been explored. Research on the potential biasing effects of survey procedures has begun, and the effects on the quality and quantity of answers and on return rates are being studied (Jones and Lang, 1980). This work has little theoretical grounding.

Predictions from the theories of Triandis (1977, 1980) and Rothchild (1979a, 1979b) and from the work on functional theory by McKillip and Lockhart (in press) suggest that interactions between survey procedure and respondent type should be expected to be the rule, not the exception. The prospect of differential attrition from evaluation groups, especially in quasi-experimental designs or where the program sponsor is also the survey sponsor, suggests that evaluators should be cautious in the use of mailed surveys and that they need to be sensitive to the possible biasing effect of survey procedures. Detailed examination for the presence of differential attrition (St. Pierre and Proper, 1978), should be routine practice in all evaluation.

The purpose of this chapter was to suggest theoretical approaches to research on the use of mailed questionnaires, an area in which there has been little theoretical application. The four theories that have been reviewed by no means cover all the theoretical applications that could be made. Indeed, two theories that receive some discussion in the literature—cognitive dissonance and social exchange—have been ignored. However, the theories reviewed here, especially those of Triandis (1977, 1980) and Rothchild (1979a, 1979b), provide a rich and somewhat contradictory set of hypotheses to guide users of mailed questionnaires. Without such guidance, the literature on this technique will continue to wander in a purely empirical wasteland, and the hidden costs of various attempts to increase return rates will remain hidden.

References

Ajzen, I., and Fishbein, M. "Attitude-Behavior Relations: A Theoretical Analysis and Review of Empirical Research." *Psychological Bulletin*, 1977, *84*, 889–918.

Ajzen, I., and Fishbein, M. *Understanding Attitudes and Predicting Social Behavior.* Englewood Cliffs, N.J.: Prentice-Hall, 1980.

Bem, D. "Self-Perception Theory." In L. Berkowitz (Ed.), *Advances in Experimental Social Psychology*, 1972, *6*, 2–62.

Berkowitz, L., and Walster, E. (Eds.). "Equity Theory: Toward a General Theory of Social Interaction." *Advances in Experimental Social Psychology*, 1976, *7*.

Dillman, D. *Mail and Telephone Surveys: The Total Design Method.* New York: Wiley-Interscience, 1978.

Fishbein, M. "A Theory of Reasoned Action: Some Applications and Implications." In M. M. Page (Ed.), *Nebraska Symposium on Motivation 1979.* Lincoln: University of Nebraska Press, 1980.

Fishbein, M., and Ajzen, I. *Belief, Attitude, Intentions and Behavior: An Introduction to Theory and Research.* Boston: Addison-Wesley, 1976.

Furse, D. H., and Stewart, D. W. "Monetary Incentives Versus Promised Contributions to Charity: New Evidence on Mailed Survey Response." *Journal of Marketing Research*, 1982, *19*, 375–380.

Heberlein, T. A., and Baumgartner, R. "Factors Affecting Response Rates to Mailed Questionnaires: A Quantitative Analysis of the Published Literature." *American Sociological Review*, 1978, *43*, 447–462.

Houston, M. J., and Nevin, J. R. "The Effect of Source and Appeal on Mailed Survey Response Patterns." *Journal of Marketing Research*, 1977, *14*, 374–378.

Hovland, C. I., Janis, I. L., and Kelley, H. H. *Communication and Persuasion.* New Haven, Conn.: Yale University Press, 1953.

Jones, W. H., and Lang, J. R. "Sample Composition Bias and Response Bias in Mail Surveys: A Comparison of Inducement Methods." *Journal of Marketing Research*, 1980, *17*, 69–76.

Katz, S. "The Functional Approach to Attitude Change." *Public Opinion Quarterly*, 1960, *24*, 163–204.

Kelman, H. C. "Compliance, Identification, and Internalization: Three Processes of Attitude Change." *Journal of Conflict Resolution*, 1958, *2*, 51–60.

Linsky, A. S. "Stimulating Responses to Mailed Questionnaires: A Review." *Public Opinion Quarterly*, 1975, *38*, 82–101.

Lockhart, D. C. Personal communication. 1983.

McKillip, J., and Lockhart, D. C. "Effectiveness of Cover Letter Appeals." *Journal of Social Psychology*, 1984, *122*, 85–91.

Rothchild, M. L. "Advertising Strategies for High- and Low-Involving Situations." In J. C. Maloney and B. Silverman (Eds.), *Attitude Research Plays for High Stakes.* American Marketing Association, 1979a.

Rothchild, M. L. "Marketing Communications in Nonbusiness Situations: Or, Why It's So Hard to Sell Brotherhood Like Soap." *Journal of Marketing*, 1979b, *43*, 11–20.

Sherif, C. W. "Social Values, Attitudes, and the Involvement of Self." In M. M. Page (Ed.), *Nebraska Symposium on Motivation 1979.* Lincoln: University of Nebraska Press, 1980.

St. Pierre, R. G., and Proper, E. C. "Attrition." *Evaluation Quarterly,* 1978, *2,* 52–71.

Triandis, H. C. *Interpersonal Behavior.* Monterey, Calif.: Brooks/Cole, 1977.

Triandis, H. C. "Values, Attitudes, and Interpersonal Behavior." In M. M. Page (Ed.), *Nebraska Symposium on Motivation 1979.* Lincoln: University of Nebraska Press, 1980.

Wicker, A. W. "Attitudes Versus Actions: The Relationship of Verbal and Overt Behavioral Responses to Attitude Objects." *Journal of Social Issues,* 1969, *25,* 41–75.

Yu, J., and Cooper, H. "A Quantitative Review of Research Design Effects on Response Rates to Questionnaires." *Journal of Marketing Research,* 1983, *20,* 36–44.

Jack McKillip is an associate professor in the Department of Psychology at Southern Illinois University at Carbondale.

*The editor describes stages at which the evaluator can reduce
the resistance of potential respondents to mailed questionnaires.*

The Stages of Mailed Questionnaire Returning Behavior

Daniel C. Lockhart

Why do people complete and return mailed evaluation questionnaires? This
question is often asked by researchers and authors. Usually, the best answer
that they can give is to cite a study, which may or may not agree with another
study. What is the researcher to do when the empirical data are contradictory?
Regression approaches to literature reviews solve this problem by averaging
the effects. If the statistician is knowledgeable and there are sufficient data, then
interaction variables can be introduced into the equation. However, to inter-
pret a set of data, a theory is needed that explains interactions and that enables
us to make sense of seeming chaos when the research data are incomplete.

Since the primary researchers in the areas of evaluation and mailed
questionnaires represent preparadigmatic sciences (sociology, psychology,
political science), a theory in this area may be premature at this time. According to Kuhn (1970), an awareness of anomalies plays an important part in the
development of theories. The literature on mailed questionnaires indicates that
the scientists in this area are aware of the inability of theory to explain com-

I am grateful to the following people for their comments on earlier drafts of this
chapter: Jim Alstchuld, Michael Lower, J. Robert Russo, Jack McKillip, Don
Dillman, Hal Strasel, Seward Smith, and Kathy Buckner. In addition, I would like to
acknowledge the editorial assistance of Ernest House, Michael C. Troutman, and Paul
McKeown.

D. C. Lockhart (Ed.). *Making Effective Use of Mailed Questionnaires.*
New Directions for Program Evaluation, no. 21. San Francisco: Jossey-Bass, March 1984.

pletely what we see in the research. Moreover, there seems to be little understanding of the behaviors that must occur for an accurately completed questionnaire to be returned.

This chapter outlines these behaviors in the hope that by better understanding these behaviors we can begin to understand the research results that we have been seeing. In this chapter, I hypothesize six stages that define the behavior of returning mailed questionnaires. I describe these behaviors, and I provide information that can help researchers to use mailed questionnaires. Further research on each of these behaviors can help to produce a unifying theory of mailed questionnaire behaviors. No theory of mailed questionnaire behavior will be complete unless all these behaviors are explained. The end result will be a theoretical framework that allows us to design questionnaires that meet the needs of various populations, research topics, and organizations. We all know that certain techniques are successful in obtaining responses to mailed surveys, but a theory would tell us why these techniques work. By outlining these behaviors, we can develop a theory of these behaviors that will answer questions about why they occur.

A completed mailed questionnaire is not the sole aim of a researcher who is conducting a mail survey. He or she also requires the questionnaire to be completed accurately by a representative sample of subjects. Therefore, it is necessary not only to sum the behaviors to conduct a proper mailed questionnaire but also to determine whether there are some interactions that degrade the quality of data. For example, if a technique that increases the return rate at one stage causes answers to be biased at a later stage, then that technique may be successful in increasing the return rate, but it is undesirable in view of the aims of the entire survey. Many questions regarding the interaction of variables cannot now be answered.

The State of the Art

For many years, return rates have been a primary dependent variable in research on mailed questionnaires. This work on return rates has been very valuable to practitioners, and it will probably continue to be influential in the development of theory. However, work like that reported by Sudman and Bradburn in this volume adds an important new dimension to study in this area. The combination of work on return rates and work on accuracy of responses offers the current practitioner data that are important both for designing new questionnaires and for understanding data collected with this methodology.

The authors of the chapters in this volume have contributed significantly to practice or research on the use of mailed questionnaires in program evaluation. Some of this work has been in applied areas, and some of this work has been in academic areas. The work of the authors represents the forefront of current effort to understand the behaviors involved in the return of mailed questionnaires.

Chapters One and Four suggest that the researcher's attention to detail somehow facilitates the desired behavior. This seems to indicate that some aspect of (correlate of?) the researcher's involvement in the process is somehow transferred to potential respondents. Potential respondents probably do not have a cognition that is related to the researcher's attention to detail. Their thoughts are probably more closely related to how they feel about the particular survey or about surveys in general. It seems likely that the researcher's attention to detail somehow makes the process of returning the completed questionnaire more rewarding for potential respondents. It is probably rewarding for a person who completes the questionnaire and neutral or negative in feeling for a person who does not complete the questionnaire. However, some individuals appear to perceive questionnaire-returning behavior as an issue of reducing the punishing consequences. Therefore, there must be something (or some set of variables) that is more positive about completing a mailed questionnaire than about not completing it, although neither consequence appears to be very severe. If we assume that behavior occurs as a result of anticipated rewards or avoidance of punishment, then it is the researcher's job to facilitate positive cognitions of completing the quesionnaire. In this chapter, I will describe six stages at which these types of cognitions appear to be important.

The Six Stages of Returning Behavior

This chapter defines several separate behaviors — qualitatively different areas for research — that together result in the completion and return of a mailed questionnaire. Research in any one of these stages probably would not result in a theory of mailed questionnaire returning behavior. It is only by understanding all the stages separately and in combination that a comprehensive theory of mailed questionnaire returning behavior is likely to result.

The six stages described here are analogous in at least one manner to the stages of human development discussed by Piaget (1950) and Erikson (1950). To start any particular stage, it is necessary for the preceding stage to have been completed. In addition, the order in which one progresses through these stages is relatively inflexible. However, due to the level of cognitive involvement, the learning or environmental component of these stages is probably stronger than it is in the stages of early human development. In addition, it seems likely that some individuals complete all the stages within minutes, while other individuals take considerably longer to complete just one.

Stage One: Receiving the Questionnaire. The first stage as conceptualized in this chapter is the mailing stage. This first stage includes the acquisition of an appropriate mailing list and the mailing of the questionnaires. A number of events occur at this stage, but most of the errors that cause a questionnaire not to be returned have little to do with the cognitions of potential respondents. Most of these problems occur because the potential respondent has a neutral cognition (no awareness) of completing the questionnaire. The researcher must establish some type of link through the mail to assist the recipient in completing the stage of receiving the questionnaire.

If the questionnaire is not received, the questionnaire cannot be completed and returned. At this stage, the potential respondent does not have many choices. If the mail is received, he or she can pick up the questionnaire or not. If he or she refuses the mail, then the remaining stages cannot be completed. The chapter by Sudman and Bradburn in this volume and other work (Bradburn and Sudman, 1979) suggest that the aged and the less educated are inappropriate for sampling using the mailed questionnaire methodology. There are two ways of interpreting this suggestion: These populations may be less likely to receive the mail for want of a forwarding address or because the addressee is ill or dead. Or, these populations fail to complete and return the questionnaire because their members fail to pass one of the subsequent stages.

Many researchers may not recognize receiving the questionnaire as an appropriate stage, owing to its lack of similarity with the following stages. However, this stage represents an important area in which many questionnaire designers fail because they do not reduce resistance of potential respondents to completing the questionnaire. The recipient's total lack of awareness of the questionnaire at this stage (if the questionnaire is not received) represents a major hurdle for researchers. Selection of an inappropriate sample is another failing at this stage, but the solution to that problem is more appropriately discussed in a volume on sampling.

Stage Two: Opening the Mail. At the second stage, the basic question is, "Does the individual open the questionnaire, or does he or she discard it, pass it on to someone else, or keep it?" The individual's response to this stimulus probably depends on perceptual processes related to the appearance of this mail. Does the recipient like the color of the mail? Is the organization one with which he or she is familiar? Has this organization or one like it sent junk mail before? Who is sending this mail?

This stage has received little direct attention in the literature on mailed questionnaires. Few studies have manipulated any variable to determine whether the recipient opens the mailed questionnaire. Dillman's (1978) Total Design Method recommends several techniques that probably have their impact at this stage: The use of letterhead and the day of mailing are two things that Dillman mentions. However, controlled studies of the relative impact of letterhead and no letterhead have not been reported. The absence of such studies could have several explanations: The variable may have no effect. There may be no journal for research on this variable. The chapter by Dillman and colleagues in this volume suggests that a full set of response-inducing techniques may have far more impact that any single technique.

Theories in the area of perception appear to be important for understanding the process of completing stage two. There is no doubt that research in the area of opening one's mail will begin the process of understanding this stage. Studies that describe techniques for obtaining a high response rate offer some suggestions about the variables that are important in completing this stage. In addition, studies that demonstrate effects of foot-in-the-door techniques, individual differences, and sponsorship of research offer other suggestions about issues related to this stage.

The relevant research addresses such variables as personalization and subject. In addition, such techniques as stick-on computer labels or individually typed labels and sending the questionnaire to office or home probably have an impact on completion of this stage. Such variables as the appearance of the questionnaire and its wording cannot have an impact at this stage. Their impact is evident only at stages three or four.

Stage Three: Forming an Overall Impression. The third stage involves some type of global or overall inspection of the questionnaire using a subject salient criterion. In contrast to the first two stages, the third stage does not seem as time-dependent. This stage is probably overcome when the recipient looks at the front page and leafs through the questionnaire. This global impression is followed by a decision to complete the questionnaire or not to complete it. If the recipient decides to complete the questionnaire, then he or she must decide whether to sit down and complete it on the spot or whether to put it away and complete it at a later time. The recipient's decision is probably based on some type of cost-benefit analysis of the relative urgency of various tasks, including completion of the mailed questionnaire. The length of the questionnaire can be expected to have its impact at this stage, although this impact has rarely been substantiated; Chapters Three and Five address this issue.

The first decision at stage three — to complete or not to complete the questionnaire — appears to be related to cover letters, cover pages, and other variables that probably have an effect on this global impression. Dillman (1978) stresses the importance of cover letters in his Total Design Method, and recent work by McKillip and Lockhart (1984) seems to indicate that cover letters have a differential impact on specific populations. It appears that the researcher can reduce the resistance of potential respondents at this stage by associating the survey with some apparent concern of potential respondents.

Stage three has probably been more researched than any of the others. Such variables as incentives, personalization, and foot-in-the-door techniques all have their impact on reducing the apparent difficulty of completing this stage. A number of different variables appear to have their impact on this stage, and literature reviews and such work as that by Heberlein and Baumgartner in Chapter Five probably are best prepared to answer questions regarding interactions between variables that facilitate or debilitate the target behavior. In Chapter Four, Dillman and colleagues suggest that adherence to details of the Total Design Method (Dillman, 1978) is facilitating.

The second decision that the recipient makes at this stage does not at first glance appear to be a significant variable. If the recipient decides to complete the questionnaire (and we know that most completed questionnaires are returned within two weeks), then the recipient must decide to complete the questionnaire within two weeks. The data appear to be deceiving. As Campbell (1943) has so aptly noted, there are two types of individuals who decide to complete a questionnaire: Those who decide to and get around to it and those who decide to and do not get around to it. The second group of well-meaning potential respondents represent the group that seems to be affected by the most widespread notion in the literature on mailed questionnaires: Reminders work and more reminders work better. Perhaps we need to hypothesize a stage within stage three to represent the time in the respondent's perceptual frame at which this stage is completed.

Stage Four: Answering the Questions. After the recipient forms an over-all impression and decides to complete the questionnaire, he or she sits down to complete the questionnaire. The process of answering the questions in the questionnaire represents the fourth stage. The researcher's task in manipulating the potential at this stage is determined by what the questions are asking and by how the questions are asked. Following basic rules for writing questions reduces the resistance of potential respondents to completing this stage. There are many useful books on asking questions (Oppenheim, 1966; Payne, 1951).

The research relevant to this stage is not specific to mailed questionnaires, and it can be found in many different disciplines—psychology, sociology, political science, evaluation. Bradburn and Sudman (1979) represent some outstanding work on the asking of specific types of questions.

Assisting respondents in completing this stage is a common failing for many researchers, who have little experience in questionnaire design. Such problems as asking several questions at once and leading respondents to a desirable answer are common occurrences. My experience as a potential respondent to surveys has been not to respond to surveys that cause me difficulty when I attempt to answer the questions, except when a friend has sent me the questionnaire.

Stage Five: Returning the Questionnaire. The fifth stage is returning the completed or almost completed questionnaire. Although this stage is frequently determined by the potential respondent at stage three—most individuals who complete a questionnaire probably return it—it is discussed as stage five because of the time at which the behavior occurs and because of the previous stages have to be passed before it can happen.

The problem that respondents encounter in completing this stage include incriminating or objectionable questions, requests for donations by the researchers, and lack of a convenient means to return the questionnaire. Most respondents probably decide not to complete stage five in the process of deciding to approach stage four. If no stamped addressed return envelope is included with the questionnaire, these individuals decide not to answer the questions as part of their overall impression of the questionnaire. Other facilitating conditions also probably have their impact when the potential respondent has completed stage four; there must be some strong punishing though that overcomes the dissonance that would result from not returning a mailed questionnaire that the individual has taken time to complete.

At this stage, the environment seems to favor the desired response. It is probably a very rare occurrence that someone completes all the previous stages and does not complete this stage. Only the researcher who places some large obstacle between the respondent who has completed the questionnaire and the mailbox in which the questionnaire belongs fails to assist the respondent in completing this stage.

Stage Six: Dealing with Nonrespondents. A special case includes those individuals whom Campbell (1943) refers to as people who intend to respond but never get around to it. These people probably include all the individuals who are assisted by a reminder. The literature on reminders is probably the least disputed in this area: Reminders work, and more reminders work better. The people in this group can probably be subdivided into those who get around to it after reminder one, those who get around to it after reminder two, and those who get around to it after reminder three. Since research on sending replacement questionnaires with reminders has been inconclusive, reminders probably have little effect on the dedicated nonrespondent who discards the questionnaire on receipt.

While it is known that some techniques work, it is not known why they work. Reminders fall into this category. Owing to the reduction on N size that occurs when one reaches the stage of sending reminders and to the practical concerns of obtaining a high response rate, little is known about why reminders work. It appears that any theory concerning why reminders work must mention the individuals who intend to respond and never get around to it. Perhaps those in this group include all the individuals who respond to reminders.

Conclusions

The conceptualization discussed in this chapter represents six major stages for which the researcher must provide incentives if potential respondents are to complete a mailed questionnaire. These stages occur at points where the potential respondent is forced to have some type of cognition. This cognition is likely to be some variant of three levels: punishing, rewarding, or neutral. A neutral conceptualization and a punishing conceptualization both cause the questionnaire not to be completed. The potential respondent must view each stage of the completion process as one of moving either toward a reward or away from a punishment. The researcher wishes to reduce the resistance of potential respondents to accomplish all the stages.

The first stage consists of receiving the questionnaire. If this stage results in anything less than receipt of a questionnaire, then the researcher did not overcome the potential respondent's resistance to completing this stage. An inaccurate address causes the questionnaire to go to another address, and a neutral—that is, no—response from the intended respondent is the result. There appears to be no negative response that can occur at this stage. Either condition, neutral or negative, results in an incomplete questionnaire.

The second stage consists of opening the mail. If both stage one and stage two are not overcome, then the recipient will not respond to the questionnaire. Furthermore, if stage one is not completed, then stage two cannot be completed. This implies that any time when a researcher does not accomplish the task of reducing the resistance of a potential respondent to completing both stage one and stage two, then the questionnaire will not be returned. Stage two does not necessarily imply close examination of the envelope, but some acknowledgement of the sender probably occurs before the recipient opens the envelope.

The researcher must accomplish different tasks to reduce the resistance of potential respondents to completing each stage. Perhaps different theories explain the behavior of respondents at each stage. The researcher can use qualitatively different techniques to assist potential respondents in completing each stage. Table 1 is a tabular representation of these stages together with a few relevant known techniques and a few relevant areas of current research.

Different measurement processes need to be used to understand which theories (or techniques) are useful in assisting potential respondents to complete each stage. For example, the researcher may have some difficulty in measuring failures to complete stage one. If questionnaires are mailed at bulk rates, then the researcher may not know how many incorrect addresses were in the mailing list. If knowledge of incorrect addresses is a necessary part of the study, then the savings that result from use of bulk mail may need to be weighed against the knowledge gained about nonrespondents that first-class mail brings.

Table 1. Stages of Mailed Questionnaire Behavior, Techniques Which Effect These Behaviors, and Research Areas of Theoretical Importance

Stage	Techniques	Research Area
Receiving the questionnaire	Accurate samples Accurate addresses	Sampling
Opening the mail	Organizational affiliation Subject sample	Business Perception
Forming an overall impression	Salience of topic Length of questionnaire	Perception Social psychology
Answering the questions	Proper questions Proper organization	Social psychology Scaling Measurement
Returning the questionnaire	Return envelopes Return postage	Business Sociology
Dealing with nonrespondents	Reminders Additional contacts	Mailed questionnaires Sampling

The answer to the question, Why do individuals complete and return questionnaires? will ultimately provide the needed theory. This answer will address many factors discussed in the various chapters of this volume. The theory will probably have to include individual difference components as well as situational components. In other words, it may be that some individuals are people who return questionnaires and that other individuals are people who do not return questionnaires. Moreover, most people who return questionnaires probably do not return every questionnaire that they receive. Therefore, each individual has a variability across circumstances and situations that influences his or her returning and completing behavior. Both individual differences in a person's normal (average, expected) behavior and situational differences that alter that person's normal behavior appear to be important factors in any understanding that we will reach of this behavior.

The Future

Regardless of the results of researcher's attempts to develop a theory of mailed questionnaire returning behavior, it can be hoped that this volume will serve two purposes: that it will assist future evaluators in thinking about the design of their mailed questionnaires and that it will create discussion and debate that will lead to the development of an acceptable theory in this area. Mailed questionnaires can be used to gather persuasive data for both evaluative and research purposes. Currently, there is no journal or professional society whose primary mission is to integrate all the research in this area. Certainly, any attempt at such integration can only have a favorable impact on the future of survey research.

Currently, mail is used for absentee ballots in elections, and it also is used by many elected officials to obtain opinions from their constituents. Such uses represent a cost-effective means of collecting many types of important data in a democratic government. Many elections could be run at a considerable savings to the taxpayer by use of the mail. If the mailed questionnaire methodology were used in conjunction with current election procedures, it could cause both the sample of the population that voted to become more representative and the turnout for elections to increase.

As Russo points out in Chapter Two, there may be many other new and successful uses of this methodology that have not been explored to date. We can hope that the work aimed at increasing our understanding of this methodology will continue. Creative efforts will be needed to broaden our understanding. However, precisely such an understanding of the issues related to this methodology is necessary if we are to use it properly. Currently, there are many abusers of the method, and they have given it a bad name. The research community of this nation should not deride the methodology because it has been poorly used by a few. The authors of the chapters in this volume represent only a small proportion of those who are struggling to perfect the methodology and to use it optimally. It is to be hoped that this volume will acquaint other evaluators with the issues that need to be considered in designing a mailed evaluation questionnaire. This methodology can be a potent data collection tool for evaluators if it is used properly.

References

Bradburn, N. M., and Sudman, S. *Improving Interview Method and Questionnaire Design: Response Effects to Threatening Questions in Survey Research.* San Francisco: Jossey-Bass, 1979.

Campbell, D. T. "Bias in Mail Surveys." *Public Opinion Quarterly,* 1943.

Dillman, D. A. *Mail and Telephone Surveys: The Total Design Method.* New York: Wiley-Interscience, 1978.

Erikson, E. H. *Childhood and Society.* New York: W. W. Norton, 1950.

Kuhn, T. S. *The Structure of Scientific Revolutions.* (2nd ed.) Chicago: University of Chicago Press, 1970.

McKillip, J., and Lockhart, D. C. "The Effectiveness of Cover-Letter Appeals." *The Journal of Social Psychology,* 1984, *122,* 85–91.

Oppenheim, A. N. *Questionnaire Design and Attitude Measurement.* New York: Basic Books, 1966.

Payne, S. L. *The Art of Asking Questions.* Princeton, N.J.: Princeton University Press, 1951.

Piaget, J. *The Psychology of Intelligence.* London: Routledge and Kegan Paul, 1950.

Daniel C. Lockhart is a research analyst at Hi-tech Systems, Inc., Columbus, Georgia.

Index